LEAD LIKE
A MARINE

LEAD LIKE A MARINE

Run Towards a Challenge, Assemble Your Fireteam, and Win Your Next Battle

John Warren and John Thompson

HARPER
BUSINESS

An Imprint of HarperCollinsPublishers

HarperCollins books may be purchased for educational, business, or sales promotional use. For information, please email the Special Markets Department at SPsales@harpercollins.com.

FIRST EDITION

Designed by Nancy Singer

Library of Congress Cataloging-in-Publication Data

Names: Warren, John (JW), author.
Title: Lead like a marine : run towards a challenge, assemble your fireteam, and win your next battle / John Warren & John Thompson.
Description: First edition. | New York, NY : HarperCollins Publishers, [2023] | Includes index.
Identifiers: LCCN 2022060238 (print) | LCCN 2022060239 (ebook) | ISBN 9780063264373 (hardcover) | ISBN 9780063264380 (ebk)
Subjects: LCSH: Leadership. | Resilience (Personality trait) | Success in business.
Classification: LCC HD57.7 .W375 2023 (print) | LCC HD57.7 (ebook) | DDC 658.4/092—dc23/eng/20230426
LC record available at https://lccn.loc.gov/2022060238
LC ebook record available at https://lccn.loc.gov/2022060239

23 24 25 26 27 LBC 5 4 3 2 1

This book is dedicated to the Marines of Lima Company, Third Battalion, Eighth Marines—especially to those who made the ultimate sacrifice in Iraq or Afghanistan. *Semper fi.*

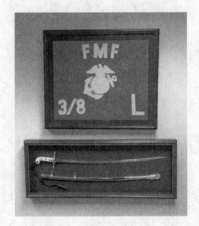

CONTENTS

Contents

PART III
PUTTING IT ALL TOGETHER

INTRODUCTION

Throwing Out the Traditional Playbook

Like many veterans who leave the Marine Corps, we were not a natural fit for corporate America, with its tendency towards office politics and overcaution, and its chronic undervaluing of common sense, strategic focus, and true teamwork. We both felt restless and frustrated during our brief experiences at traditionally run companies. So we started our own business and set out to run it very differently, in every possible way—from hiring, training, and culture to operations, sales, customer service, and more.

By the fall of 2013, Lima One Capital was doing well for a two-year-old startup, especially one led by two guys who had started with no experience or connections in real estate finance. We were originating about $3 million in loans every month, with ambitions to expand beyond our first three states of South Carolina, North Carolina, and Georgia. But taking Lima One to the next level would require hundreds of millions in additional capital, an order of magnitude beyond our resources at the time. That's why we had flown from our home base of Greenville, South Carolina, to Miami, for a half-hour pitch that could change everything.

Our meeting that day, arranged by one of our investment bankers, would be with the billionaire real estate mogul William C. Erbey. We had good reasons to be optimistic. With just nine employees, we were originating 74 percent of all short-term real estate investor loans in Atlanta. We had a scalable model to originate loans in any market, and a smart plan to expand into our next eighteen states. Best of all, Lima One's early loans were starting to pay off, so we could show investors a record of success. As one of our first investors had told us, "Anyone can make a loan. My five-year-old can make a loan. The question is whether it will pay off. Until investors see that your loans consistently pay off, they will be skeptical. But once you prove that you know what you're doing, they will keep coming back for more, just like addicts."

On our way to Erbey's office, our investment banker asked if we were nervous. Thinking back to the many near-death experiences we had survived during our combat deployment to Iraq, we said no, we weren't nervous. What was the worst a billionaire could do to us? Being under constant threat of death for seven months had given us a great sense of perspective.

He then warned us that it would seem arrogant and naïve if we told Erbey that our five-year goal was originating $1 billion in annual loans; projecting such massive growth would look too aggressive. This didn't make much sense to us. Why not be honest about our big ambitions, if we had a plan to back them up? But if this was how the game was played, so be it. We reluctantly agreed to sound modest if Erbey asked how big we wanted to grow.

When we got to his office, we found that Erbey had been holding meetings in thirty-minute increments all day. He was clearly a no-nonsense guy, in his beautiful designer suit, suspenders, and tie. His operational questions showed that he had read our pitch book carefully. We were well prepared with all our answers. Then, as our half-hour slot was nearly over, he said, "I'm really interested in Lima One. Just one more question—how big do you think you can get in the next five years?"

JW, eager to give a straight answer, glanced at our investment banker, who responded with a subtle head shake: *don't do it!* JW looked back to Erbey and replied, "We want to grow Lima One into a premier lending company that originates five hundred million dollars in loans annually."

At that point Erbey closed our pitch book, leaned in, and looked at us. "Well, guys, this has been a great meeting. But at my level, I can't waste my time on any business that's not aiming higher. I only invest in lenders that can originate at least one billion dollars annually."

We left empty-handed and somewhat stunned.

That was the last time we ever assumed that the traditional business playbook would be more effective than our own instincts, honed by our experiences in radically different settings. We threw that playbook away and never looked back.

Marine Corps Values in the Civilian World

The results we ultimately experienced at Lima One Capital were better than we'd ever dared to imagine. By hiring a mix of former Marines, other veterans, and lifelong civilians, and by teaching them the same principles and values that worked for us in combat, we built a team that was deeply committed, focused, creative, empowered, and energized. And we maintained all of those qualities as the staff grew from zero to 200+ over the course of a decade. The value of Lima One grew steadily as well, reaching nine figures when we were finally ready to sell it in 2019. Then we started a new company, GEM Mining, in the even more unfamiliar space of cryptocurrency. Once again, Marine-style leadership is helping us achieve rapid success, even as the crypto industry goes through dramatic ups and downs.

We wrote this book to help leaders and aspiring leaders at startups, Fortune 500 companies, nonprofits, religious and community groups, sports teams, and any other kind of organization. It's not abstract or theoretical, and mostly avoids military or business jargon. Our goal is to give you a straight-talking, practical guide to what you *really* have to do to lead like a Marine, even if you've never worn a uniform. After Part I shows you why this approach to leadership is so powerful, Part II explores the nine key strategies for leading like a Marine. We explain and illustrate them with true stories from both the Marine Corps and our businesses.

Many civilians assume that the success or failure of a military unit depends on the quality of its weapons and tactics, just as they assume that the success or failure of a business must depend on the appeal of its products. These skeptics see leadership, values, and culture as "touchy-feely" concepts that should be secondary at best, if not outright dismissed as a distraction. Maybe that's what they were taught when working for traditional companies, but they couldn't be more wrong. The "touchy-feely" stuff makes all the difference—whether you're facing a multipronged attack by heavily armed al-Qaeda insurgents, or merely trying to make your quarterly revenue goals.

After you see what we experienced in Iraq, and then in the business world, we believe you'll agree.

Notes to the Reader

To avoid any confusion between the two Johns, throughout this book we use our nicknames of JW for John Warren and Top for John Thompson. (*Top* is Marine slang for a master sergeant.) Sections labeled with those nicknames are from the perspective of just one of us.

Most of the names in this book are real, but we have occasionally changed some names and identifying details to protect people's privacy.

PART I

UNLOCKING A BETTER WAY TO LEAD

CHAPTER 1

RUN TOWARDS A CHALLENGE

Walk in Our Boots

While you don't need to be a Marine to reap the benefits of Marine-style leadership, you *will* need to walk in our boots for a while to fully understand it. So before we dig into the nine key leadership strategies, let us show you how they actually played out in combat, during a life-or-death crisis in the most dangerous city on earth.

Three years after the US invasion of Iraq deposed Saddam Hussein, Ramadi had declined from a proud and vibrant city into a focal point for anarchy. Four hundred thousand Sunnis inhabited its tightly packed mix of tall buildings and low-rise compounds. Various guerrilla factions, especially al-Qaeda, were engaged in a bloody struggle for power and posed a constant threat to US forces. Whenever we went out on a patrol, we knew that at any moment we might be blown up by an improvised explosive device (IED), shot by a sniper, or hit with a rocket-propelled grenade (RPG). Any seemingly innocent civilian might be a suicide bomber.

The 200+ members of our unit—Lima Company, Third Battalion, Eighth Marines—deployed to Ramadi in early March 2006, flying from North Carolina to Ireland, then to Kuwait, then finally into Iraq. Our mission, in the simplest terms, was to bring order to a sector in chaos.

The company that we replaced made our sector of Ramadi sound grim. They viewed the majority of Sunnis as either open or tacit al-Qaeda supporters, so those Marines defined their mission as disarming the entire population. They patrolled almost exclusively in their Humvees, because they considered foot patrols too dangerous. They counted on the higher-ups at the battalion and regiment levels to provide actionable intelligence. And when they took fire from a house or building, they often called in an air strike to obliterate the building, regardless of any collateral damage. As you'll see in upcoming chapters, Lima Company would develop a very different and much more effective counterinsurgency strategy. But first we had to get established and defend ourselves.

We divided our time between a forward operating base called Snakepit and an auxiliary building called Outpost Veterans Affairs (OPVA). In contrast to Snakepit, a well-secured area on the outskirts of the city, OPVA was a spartan, lightly defended, three-story building in the heart of Ramadi, one mile away from Snakepit. Before the war, OPVA had been an Iraqi Veterans Affairs office, but Saddam's government abandoned the building as uninhabitable after it was bombed in 2003. To the Marines, however, nothing is uninhabitable. We surrounded OPVA with walls of sandbags and concrete barriers, and Lima Company's four platoons rotated weekly duty to defend it. We had snipers on the roof 24/7 and additional Marines manning posts with heavy machine guns and grenade launchers.

By that spring of 2006, Top had been a Marine for nearly seventeen years and was on his fifth combat deployment, his third as Lima Company's gunnery sergeant. JW, in contrast, was a recently commissioned second lieutenant, commanding an infantry platoon in a combat zone for the first time. Neither of us knew that we were about to face the most violent and intense day of our entire Marine Corps careers. The story of how we came through it is a testament to the power of Marine training and leadership.

The Worst Day

April 17, 2006, started out cool and overcast, with a rare, light drizzling rain. JW began the morning by taking half of First Platoon on a routine patrol out of Snakepit. The morning prayers had just concluded on the loudspeakers of the local mosque. We were in the early stages of blanketing our sector of Ramadi with foot patrols in order to develop greater rapport and trust with local civilians. The remainder of First Platoon was still at Snakepit, along with Second and Fourth Platoons. Everything was quiet, with no signs of insurgent activity.

As JW's men were starting their patrol, Top headed out from Snakepit to oversee a resupply of OPVA, which was being manned by Third Platoon. He led about a dozen Marines who were unloading trucks with food, water, ammunition, and other essentials. While there, he planned to reinforce some defensive positions and add additional communication lines for Marines in defensive posts.

Top was on the dilapidated roof of OPVA when the morning quiet was disturbed by the sound of distant gunfire. The bursts of fire seemed more intense than usual, but that alone didn't mean much. Gunfire was the constant background noise of Ramadi, as common as traffic sounds in an American city. It didn't necessarily signify an unusual threat. Still, Top began to shift into a more alert mode.

His suspicions were soon confirmed when a squad leader for Third Platoon got a troubling report from one of his Marines at a watch post. "Traffic had died off to nothing," he recalled. "At that point in the deployment, we all knew what was about to happen." But they didn't realize that this attack wasn't typical—it was part of a much larger, coordinated attack by al-Qaeda on multiple US bases throughout Ramadi.

The sounds of enemy gunfire went from distant to close up, as several groups of insurgents began firing at OPVA with machine guns. Everyone on the roof was shooting back. Heading downstairs to coordinate with Third Platoon's commander, Top heard yells from the roof. He rushed back upstairs, finding Lance Corporal Michael Sarbu bleeding profusely, his leg bone shattered by an enemy's 7.62mm round.

It would have been easy to panic. But the men didn't, because their training kicked in. Third Platoon's Staff Sergeant Emmanuel Anglade rushed to control Lance Corporal Sarbu's bleeding with a tourniquet before evacuating him by stretcher to the third floor. There he would be stabilized by Corpsman William "Doc" Corso and given morphine until he could be evacuated from OPVA. Staff Sergeant Anglade knew the seriousness of Lance Corporal Sarbu's condition, but in typical Marine fashion, he tried to lighten the mood: "Shut up. It's just a freaking flesh wound."

Despite the jolt of adrenaline and worry caused by Lance Corporal Sarbu's injury, Top and his men were able to keep going and respond to this highly unusual crisis. For the first time in our deployment, Marines on the roof actually saw enemy machine gunners. (Before that day the insurgents had never showed their faces up close; they would use IEDs or RPGs from a distance, then hide among the civilian population.)

Then things got worse. Another wave of insurgents systematically targeted each of our six guard posts, with direct hits from RPGs. Most of the two-man teams at these posts were knocked unconscious with powerful blasts of explosives and shrapnel. Help was unreachable. When our radio operators attempted to call Snakepit for reinforcements, they found that radio communications had been cut off by the attack.

Suddenly, we had to make all our own decisions. In many organizations, this would have been a disaster, but Marines know that while centralized leadership is great for strategy, small-unit leadership ultimately wins battles. In combat, the situation evolves so fast that small-unit leaders must have the authority and the capability to make split-second decisions and show initiative. When we lost the radios, we were rattled but not defeated. That was fortunate because we were about to face an unthinkable escalation of the attack.

"I remember seeing an incredibly bright orange flash, and I didn't know if it was coming through the wall or because fire had engulfed the whole building," recalls one corporal.

Top and his men had taken cover inside OPVA, but the huge explosion threw him backward against the wall. One Marine who was thrown through the plywood door remembers thinking that "a mortar round had landed at my feet because I got thrown so far from the blast." Many Marines were injured from the blast, most unconscious with severe concussions. "I woke up basically in pitch black and feeling instantly dehydrated, like my nose was clogged," says another Marine. "My mouth was clogged. My ears were ringing. It was just complete and utter disorientation until the smoke cloud started to dissipate and the sunlight started coming through."

It was hard to imagine a worse situation. Instead of a brief engagement with a few enemies—the usual—we were facing over a hundred al-Qaeda insurgents, in an assault that would last for hours. A team on the roof could now see insurgents firing from multiple positions across the street, at both OPVA's front and rear gates. The building was surrounded and facing a coordinated, heavily armed surprise attack. We were outside our normal base, surrounded by the enemy, cut off from communication with HQ, and dealing with totally new strategies. The fireball, we'd later realize, was a suicide bomber in an explosive-packed dump truck, the first one we had encountered.

At any moment the insurgents might charge through the front door or the giant hole in the side wall created by whatever had caused that fireball. If that happened, our wounded and those treating them would be sitting ducks. And with the radio down, there was no way to know how long it would take until reinforcements arrived.

Meanwhile, two miles away at Snakepit, the explosion was loud enough to shake dust off the walls and bring every Marine running out to respond. Lima Company's commanding officer, Captain Carlos "Max" Barela, and his executive officer, Lieutenant Jason Clark, feared total devastation. "I felt the blast," recalled Clark. "At first I thought that we'd lost the whole building and everybody down there." Captain Barela saw the mushroom cloud over OPVA and thought, *I just buried a platoon.*

Despite these extraordinary circumstances, we were about to pull off a victory. At the end of the day, we would kill fifty to one hundred insurgents without losing a single Marine. How did we do it? While we had some good fortune, the key factor was the leadership choices, discipline, and habits we'd developed over months and years.

Staying Calm under Fire (Top)

Something we'd appreciate later is how much the outcome of April 17 turned on the hard work we put in before the attack. The company had invested so much time and effort into fortifying OPVA, which prevented major serious casualties when the suicide bomber detonated his bomb. Avoiding easy, comfort-based decisions before the attack yielded a huge advantage during the crisis.

Another benefit was the way Marine training helped me stay calm. I had never felt anything like that fireball exploding through the wall and into the center of OPVA. I'd been in IED attacks before, and I'd faced mortar fire, but this was very different. I assumed it was some type of missile.

Everything went silent after the blast, as Staff Sergeant Anglade and I pulled ourselves up and tried to evaluate the situation. We saw a bunch of Marines being carried to corpsmen, unconscious. We then checked the rooftop, where our four posts, manned by eight Marines, had taken heavy fire and direct RPG hits. To our amazement, all four posts had been destroyed, but every Marine was still alive. At this point, my biggest fear was that the insurgents would jump our walls and storm into OPVA, killing or capturing the majority of our Marines. I immediately ran downstairs to the main entry point and lay on the floor, preparing to fire as needed. But no one tried to charge in. Instead, the enemy continued to pound the outside of the building with hundreds of rounds from multiple machine gun positions. Marines would have pressed their advantage if the situation were reversed, but al-Qaeda chose not to run towards the danger. That would make all the difference.

Our radios inside OPVA were still down, but I knew that the command Humvee outside had a strong radio, so I decided to try running to the vehicle.

Just as I reached OPVA's garage door, another RPG exploded. I'm not ashamed to admit that I was scared shitless. I remember thinking, *This is it, I'm about to get killed out in the open.* But all of my training had taught me how to stay calm under fire. I ran to the Humvee and climbed in without being hit. Turning the knob and holding down the talk button, I said, "Snakepit, this is Lima Seven, come in Snakepit." A steady voice responded, "Go ahead, Lima Seven." It was Lieutenant Clark, who was running combat operations and firmly in control of the situation. He told me that JW's platoon was on the way, but it might take them a while to reach us if they encountered enemy fire.

As I ran back inside OPVA, my main goal was making sure no one breached the outside barrier. Staff Sergeant Anglade rounded up every available Marine from Third Platoon. Lieutenant Andrew Sherman, commander of Third Platoon, showed true poise under fire and helped direct those Marines into ad hoc rifle positions. I said, "Our mission is to make sure no one gets inside this building. This is our last stand if necessary." They began to return fire against the insurgents. At that point we received a positive jolt of energy. Captain Barela came over the now-restored OPVA radio with an unforgettable, inspiring message: "If it's not American, it dies today."*

---

* Of course he was referring to insurgents, not Iraqi civilians.

Teamwork under Fire (JW)

After concluding our routine patrol, my Marines and I ran into a surprisingly huge number of civilians clogging the main road leading to Snakepit, which we called Route Michigan. All four lanes were filled with pedestrians and traffic fleeing the city, for no apparent reason. After fighting our way through, we pulled into Snakepit for debriefing, then saw a ton of smoke from the direction of OPVA. The command center told us that OPVA was under heavy attack and an unknown number of Marines—maybe all of them—had suffered serious casualties.

First Platoon was the designated quick reaction force (QRF) that day, so I was ordered to lead our entire forty-two-man platoon to OPVA. Each of our two sections had four large Humvees, each with a heavy weapon and gunner in the turret, a driver, a vehicle commander, and one or two Marines in the backseats. Because Marine organizations are often split up into small fireteams, all of my men had experience operating with great independence and authority on their own. That is why I felt totally comfortable tasking my second section, led by my platoon sergeant, to head straight into OPVA and carry out casualty evacuations. I planned to follow with my first section to counterattack the insurgents laying siege outside.

All of First Platoon raced out of Snakepit to engage the enemy.

Just as we got about five hundred meters down Route Michigan, a parked vehicle loaded full of explosives detonated right next to our lead Humvee. As the fireball exploded into the air, I recall thinking, *I just lost four Marines*. One team leader also thought it was a catastrophic kill, recalling, "The entire vehicle just disappeared. The insurgents timed it perfectly." But after ten seconds that felt like eternity, we saw that all four Marines had made it out of the smoking wreck of the Humvee, though three were wounded.

Insurgents were now firing at both sections of our platoon in another coordinated attack. I decided to leave the remaining three Humvees from second section at that spot to treat and evacuate the casualties and return fire at the insurgents. One of our Navy corpsmen ran straight to the wounded, despite a lot of gunfire whizzing overhead, while first section and I continued to OPVA. Only five minutes into this engagement, my platoon's fighting strength was cut in half.

As we got closer, we saw that OPVA was under fire from many different angles—an unprecedented, sustained attack. April 17 was the first time we actually saw groups of insurgents standing and facing us. They were dressed in all black, knit clothes, with masks and sneakers. They looked like a cross between the Viet Cong and American kids dressed like ninjas for Halloween. All carried AK-47s, and some also had grenades or RPGs.

With only four Humvees left, I ordered two to go inside OPVA and evacuate casualties, while mine and one other would counterattack from outside. I ordered my driver to stop just east of OPVA. Using his M240 machine gun from his turret position, one Marine opened fire on the attacking insurgents to the south. Lance Corporal Ryan Garner and I got out and tried to use the hood of the Humvee as partial cover, as we began firing on the same insurgents. I had an M4 with an M203 grenade launcher attached. Lance Corporal Garner rained hell down on them with his M32 semiautomatic grenade launcher, a fearsome weapon that looks like something Sylvester Stallone would carry in *Rambo*. Lance Corporal Garner recalls hitting "at least six insurgents, probably more. I'll never forget seeing their arms and legs go flying over the wall. It was very satisfying."

The sound of weapons firing was so loud that we couldn't hear our radios. I later found out that the section leader in the other Humvee was yelling through his intercom, warning us about more insurgents approaching from the north, behind us. We were exposed and didn't see them because we were firing to the south. These new insurgents opened automatic fire on us, their bullets bouncing off our Humvee in all directions. Lance Corporal Garner recalls, "I didn't even hear the first round, but I could feel the pressure from it. Then I heard another one, and another. I could hear the ping when the next one hit me."

Lance Corporal Garner went down hard. With so much heavy gear on, it was hard to lift him up into the Humvee, as the shooting continued without pause. When we finally got him inside, we drove for two minutes into OPVA and checked his wounds. As we removed his combat vest and flak jacket, we didn't see any blood. The round had directly hit Lance Corporal Garner's body armor, called a SAPI plate. He would be sore but only bruised.

One Cohesive Unit

Meanwhile, the rest of Lima Company was functioning as one cohesive unit, with leaders of all ranks showing initiative. At Snakepit the Marine in charge of base security reinforced his defensive posts with additional Marines. As insurgent small-arms fire escalated against Snakepit, Fourth Platoon fiercely defended the base and returned fire.

Simultaneously, the second section of First Platoon was still on Route Michigan, inspecting other suspicious parked cars that might be packed with explosives. Lance Corporal Blair Paton remembers one car "sitting heavy in the back end. It seemed to be loaded down. So I stepped out and fired a grenade from about a hundred and twenty yards away." As he suspected, that car blew up like a fireworks factory. More than half of the other cars parked on Route Michigan were also rigged up as IEDs and had to be safely detonated.

Back inside OPVA, Third Platoon ran the urgent casualty evacuation of Lance Corporal Sarbu and other wounded Marines into First Platoon's Humvees, as the attack continued.

Sergeant Camden MacGregor then led the vehicles with the wounded down a bullet-ridden Route Michigan, speeding "like a scene from *Dukes of Hazzard*." Ten minutes later he pulled into Camp Ramadi, which housed the nearest US trauma center. Though Lance Corporal Sarbu had told people he expected to die of his wounds, he found his sense of humor when meeting his surgeon: "Hey, keep an eye on this guy. He's got a Red Sox cap! I don't want him to kill me if he knows I'm a Yankees fan." The

Navy surgeon replied, "Don't worry about it, we'll take care of you. Just know that you're going to owe your life to a Red Sox fan!"

After dropping off the wounded, Sergeant MacGregor received word that Third Platoon was short on ammo back at OPVA. He gave the order to his Marines: "If you ain't shot, get back in the trucks." They returned to Snakepit for a "smash and grab" to get more ammo, then raced back down Route Michigan. He describes the scene on the road: "Just Armageddon. Columns of smoke, burning cars. There were bodies. It was chaos."

Corporal Kyle Herl sums up the impact of having a cohesive unit driven by powerful values: "There was no hesitation on the part of anybody. Everyone just started doing what they needed to do. There was zero selfishness. We all showed up and got it done."

Leadership When the Shooting Stops (Top)

JW and I discussed the situation when he got to OPVA, before he led his two Humvees back outside to rejoin the fight. Al-Qaeda's hesitance to advance and the tenacity of JW's men fighting their way to our rescue had turned the tide. For about two hours—an eternity in modern combat—the battle raged as the insurgents continued to hit us with machine guns and RPGs. But then they finally gave up and withdrew.

For several hours after the insurgents retreated, both sections of JW's platoon made repeated resupply trips between Snakepit and OPVA. They also helped me and the other Marines begin to rebuild the defenses around the building. While they were there, someone snapped a picture of the IED damage to second section's lead vehicle.

During one of those resupply runs, the enemy set off yet another IED on Route Michigan, this time right next to JW's own Humvee. Remarkably, no one was seriously injured by the resulting fireball, and they managed to limp back to the relative safety of Snakepit.

Meanwhile, we took a closer look at the blast site at OPVA, and I realized it hadn't been a missile attack after all—it was worse. A large dump truck, loaded with explosives, had broken through the side gate

Private First Class Boyd Smith and Lance Corporal David Byers standing in front of their Humvee, which had been hit by a vehicle-borne IED on April 17, 2006.

of OPVA and detonated against our side wall. In the propaganda video later released by al-Qaeda, you can see hundreds of tracer rounds from Third Platoon Marines zinging off that dump truck. But because the truck was armored, and higher-ups at battalion had denied our request for armor-piercing ammo, it couldn't be stopped before the explosion.

We later found out that the suicide driver was a Saudi national, recruited by Abu Musab al-Zarqawi, the leader of al-Qaeda in Iraq. This meant that al-Qaeda was now desperate enough to send suicide bombers against us, in addition to ground fighters with machine guns, IEDs, and RPGs. There might be another all-out assault when we least expected it.

We immediately began repairing the breached wall and reinforcing the building's security perimeter, and a team of Army engineers inspected OPVA that night. "They told us the building might fall down and we should evacuate," Lieutenant Sherman recalls. "I replied that there's no chance in hell I'm going to give the enemy the satisfaction of driving us away." Instead of evacuating OPVA, Lima Company would keep reinforcing it with sandbags for days to come.

Before lights-out that night I typed up some notes, so I could remember the details of the hardest day of my many years in the Marines. I was tough on myself in those notes. Had I missed some red flags signaling a possible attack in the days or weeks prior? How did the enemy get so close before we spotted them? What could we have done better to prepare? Why weren't our rooftop posts more fortified? And so on.

But then I started to focus on the positives. None of our Marines had been killed, and we were able to evacuate the wounded for treatment. Most important, we didn't give up. We stayed calm under fire and quickly planned and executed a response. We took the fight to the enemy and went after them aggressively, for as long as it took to drive them away. We estimated that Lima Company killed between fifty and one hundred insurgents that day, while they killed zero Marines. We didn't let them destroy OPVA, and we damn sure wouldn't let them chase us away. In fact, about seven weeks later we would transfer Snakepit to the Iraqi Army, and Lima Company would live full-time at OPVA for the rest of our deployment.

The modern corporate world tends to emphasize safety. While that is an important goal in some scenarios, strong organizations should be staffed with people who run towards a challenge, not away from it. When you go through challenging times together and succeed together, that's what builds a strong culture, on any kind of team. It's never some bullshit rah-rah speech from a leader or coach. Because almost everyone in Lima Company was part of the fight that day, one way or another, I knew that April 17 would make the company even more cohesive.

The Best Day (JW)

Later that night, Gunnery Sergeant John Gallagher, a very seasoned combat Marine, warned me that I'd probably find it impossible to sleep,

Remains of the insurgent dump truck that was detonated on OPVA by a suicide driver on April 17, 2006.

with all the adrenaline pumping from my first real combat experience. He reassured me: "No worries. Job well done." I went to my bunk, watched an episode of *Lost* to try to relax, and said my prayers.

Before falling into a deep sleep, I remember thinking that it had been the most terrifying, chaotic, and exhausting day of my life. But it had also been the *best* day of my life. I was very proud of First Platoon and Lima Company. We had fully done our duty, confronting a ferocious enemy that tried to kill us over and over. We weren't merely a well-trained military unit. We were inspired, focused, cohesive, and fully energized to fight like hell and carry out our mission.

On a personal level, while Top had already faced tough combat many times at that point, I was still a relatively green lieutenant. April 17 proved that I really could lead men effectively under fire. Confirming that once and for all, both to myself and to my platoon, felt fantastic.

John Thompson standing inside the crater from the detonation of the suicide bomber on April 17, 2006.

From left to right: First Sergeant Marty Fenton, Gunnery Sergeant John Thompson, Staff Sergeant Emmanuel Anglade, and Captain Max Barela inspecting the damage caused by the suicide bomber attack on April 17, 2006, at OPVA.

Post-Traumatic Growth

All these years later, we both still think often about April 17—but not because it gave us post-traumatic stress disorder or anything like that. While PTSD is real and damaging to some veterans, many others (a majority, in our experience) go through an opposite phenomenon that psychologists call post-traumatic growth. For these veterans, physically or emotionally painful combat experiences give them inspirational fuel to take on future challenges in civilian life. That's what happened to us. In fact, we'd go further: our combat experiences directly impacted all our future successes in business.

If we had never faced the crucible of April 17 and the rest of our deployment in Iraq, we never would have built Lima One Capital (and later GEM Mining) the way we did. The Marine Corps gave us an unshakable, 100 percent certainty that its leadership strategies really work. We figured that if Marine-style leadership could turn 200+ diverse individuals into a tightly aligned and highly effective fighting force, even during life-or-death crises, it could probably also work for employees at a startup business.

A few years later, we would have an opportunity to test that hypothesis.

CHAPTER 2

FROM COMBAT
TO BUSINESS

We don't want to imply that Marine Corps values and leadership strategies made us instantly successful in business. Our progress was actually the opposite of instant. For the first few years we struggled with uncertainty, setbacks, external skeptics, trial and error, and the consequences of our own ignorance. Fortunately, one of the most fundamental values we learned in the Marines was to not give up just because a challenge is exceptionally tough. And as we wrote in the previous chapter, like most Marines we were naturally inclined to run towards a challenge, not away from it. Here's how our unusual transition from Marines to entrepreneurs played out.

The Bumpy Road from Lima Company to Lima One (JW)

After Lima Company's deployment to Ramadi ended, I was ordered to transfer to Weapons Company, where I was given command of an 81mm mortar platoon. Then, following a few months of additional stateside training, my platoon deployed on a Marine Expeditionary Unit (MEU) on board a Navy amphibious assault ship. The value of an MEU is that it keeps Marines on constant alert and physically close to a war zone in case they're needed on short notice. In 2007 that meant either Iraq or Afghanistan, and we were prepared to rush into combat in either country.

But over that entire seven-month deployment, no combat order ever came. The rumor was that the Pentagon didn't want to send an MEU to Afghanistan because it would look like the United States was losing. So instead of contributing to either war effort, we mostly just sailed around the Mediterranean and the Persian Gulf. I got so frustrated at this wasted opportunity that I decided to decline another term in the military. After four years, two deployments, and then a brief stint at battalion headquarters, I left the Marine Corps in June 2008.

When I got home to South Carolina with no plans or job prospects, I accepted my brother's offer to join his new social media startup, which he called GadZeus. It was a platform exclusively for fraternity and sorority members, at a time when many entrepreneurs were launching niche variations of Facebook. GadZeus would debut at each new university and see its user numbers spike quickly, because students liked it. But college administrators feared any liability stemming from fraternity and sorority chapters being able to communicate privately. They started to ban GadZeus from one campus after another, and as our user totals crashed, we burned through $300,000 in investors' money. GadZeus was a humiliating failure, but it taught me the importance of truly understanding a market before jumping in.

After GadZeus I tried to get a conventional job, but employers either ignored me or told me I lacked essential business skills. A couple of places offered me commission-only sales jobs for products I didn't respect. But I mostly heard what many veterans hear at the end of an interview: "We really admire your service. But even though we'd love to be able to offer you a position, you don't have the necessary industry experience."

At this point I had recently married my wife, Courtney, and I felt self-imposed pressure to contribute my fair share of income. Continuing to pound the pavement, I landed an interview with Gerber Taylor, a Memphis, Tennessee, investment firm founded by several veterans. At the end of a great meeting, one of them told me, "You don't have the skills to work here yet, but if you get into business school, we'll hire you for the summer. Then we'll hire you full-time after you finish your MBA." I told them I'd consider their offer, but the thought of two years in business school wasn't appealing.

As I was walking out, one of the partners, a former Navy SEAL named Bill Ryan, pulled me aside. "I didn't want to contradict my partners, but you don't need an MBA. You need to go into real estate investing, where ninety-nine percent of the people don't think strategically. All they do is follow the current trends, adding more and more leverage until the market crashes. Then they blame the market. If you're not stupid or reckless, in this depressed market you can build a sustainable business." I will forever be indebted to Bill, a stranger who changed my life.

I had always loved real estate. Even before going into the Marines, I'd bought, renovated, and flipped two investment properties with my brother. Mastering real estate finance sounded exciting. When I discussed it with Courtney, she couldn't have been more supportive. She offered to keep covering our expenses from her salary while I tried to launch my own business.

I spent the next couple of months networking with real estate professionals, which led me to Ret Chandler, who had just sold his family business and was looking for investment opportunities. Ret agreed to meet with me at a Goldberg's Bagels off Interstate 285 in Atlanta. I wore my best Joseph A. Bank suit, which didn't fit well, and got there early. Then a guy came in who looked almost homeless—raggedy T-shirt, flip-flops, shorts, three-day beard. It was Ret. As he told me, "When you're looking for money you have to dress up. But once you have money you can dress however you want." After a two-hour meeting, Ret was willing to stake my first $1 million in capital, in exchange for an 8 percent return from the proceeds of my first loan portfolio.

I had found a potentially huge opportunity: rather than underwriting mortgages for homeowners, we would focus on the 20 percent of all home sales made for investment purposes, as rental properties or fix-and-flips. The government had imposed tight new regulations on those kinds of loans after the mortgage crisis, driving most banks out of that market. This created a big opening for smart nonbank lenders.

Ret and I brought in a third partner, Tom Bates, who had run a big lending company in Atlanta geared towards real estate investors, before it went bust during the crash. Tom still had real estate investors calling him for loans, so they became our first customers. We called the new partnership WCB (the initials of our last names), and I used Ret's $1 million to underwrite short-term (nine-month) loans to Tom's customers. The good news was that all nine of my initial loans in Atlanta started to pay off, and I learned a ton about underwriting. The bad news was that Ret and Tom turned out to be untrustworthy partners.* I had to dissolve WCB within a year and start hunting for new investors to build a new company.

Lima One Capital LLC, named for my call sign in Ramadi, launched in February 2011. By that spring, thanks to my growing reputation for originating high-quality loans, I landed a couple of new investors and moved back to my hometown of Greenville. But I knew that this startup would never work if it was just me and an administrative assistant. I urgently needed a partner to help me build Lima One. Learning from my mistake with Ret and Tom, I wanted someone totally trustworthy, who shared my values, who could build and lead teams, who could master any organizational challenge, and whose strengths balanced my weaknesses.

There was only one name on my short list.

_____

*   See Chapter 10 for details.

Taking Another Big Risk (Top)

After Lima Company left Ramadi, I was promoted to Master Sergeant and named deputy director of the Marine Infantry Operations Chief Course, in charge of training senior noncommissioned officers (NCOs) for combat. That was relatively easy duty at Camp Lejeune, since I knew the subject cold. But I started to get bored after a year and began to explore private sector opportunities. In the spring of 2010, after twenty-one years in uniform, I had a quiet retirement party on a Friday afternoon. The following Monday morning I returned to Camp Lejeune—but now wearing civilian clothes and a civilian ID, for a defense contractor that happened to have its offices in the same building.

I was now the operations manager for the Infantry Immersion Trainer, overseeing realistic training for Marines deploying to Iraq or Afghanistan. I made significantly more money, worked a normal nine-to-five schedule, and could enjoy the waterfront home that my wife, Sandy, and I owned in nearby Hubert, North Carolina. I even had time to pursue my passion for fishing several times a week. Having just turned forty, with my kids a few years away from leaving the nest, I could have easily maintained this pleasant lifestyle for the next twenty-plus years.

JW and I were still in touch, though we'd landed in different states. We would occasionally get together if one of us happened to be near the other. When he told me about starting Lima One Capital, it sounded interesting, but I was skeptical. Over the next several months he'd bring up the idea of me joining his company—casually at first but with increasing seriousness. In August 2011, over grilled steaks on my porch, he laid out his vision for the company and what my role could be. A few weeks later, he was back for another pitch at Ruth's Chris Steak House in Wilmington. As he summed it up: Did I want the chance to build a new company, improve my financial status, and seriously challenge myself? Or would I rather coast at a job I had already mastered, one that was already starting to make me feel restless?

As with my original decision to join the Marines at seventeen, my gut told me to take a big risk. Sandy was supportive, but she also had to look out for her own career as an event planner. Since she had months of upcoming commitments to run large weddings almost every weekend, we decided that I'd move to South Carolina solo in January 2012. Then she'd join me that April—*if* things were going well for Lima One.

The intensity of my first few months in Greenville reminded me more of a Marine deployment than a new job. I'd taken a 50 percent pay cut and was back to living like a lance corporal at the cheapest motel I could find in town. For $190 a week it was a step above OPVA, but almost as dangerous. One Sunday, while watching my beloved New York Giants play the hated Dallas Cowboys, I opened my windows and curtains to get a bit more airflow. I soon heard a knock on my door by the security guard, who said, "Sir, it's not safe to leave your curtains and windows open here. Please close them immediately."

Meanwhile, I studied an industry that I knew very little about. Our workload was intense, with no support at first beyond one assistant, but it felt great to be building something of significance.

The Cash Crunch (JW)

When Top arrived, we had just received a new $4 million line of credit from our biggest investor, Arnie. That seemed like a huge pool of capital, but we loaned it out faster than we anticipated. We originated so many quality loans, so quickly, that by the end of March our capital was fully lent out.

This cash crunch didn't mean that we'd go bankrupt right away, but it meant we could no longer make new loans and grow. This posed a huge threat to our reputation. We'd been trying to maintain a steady flow of incoming loan applications, but if we began turning away borrowers because we were out of cash, it would be like a diner running out of eggs and coffee. Once you lose your credibility, it's very hard if not impossible to recover. We tried to stall our newest loan applicants while we looked for more capital, but that tactic wouldn't work for long. So I drove to Atlanta, hat in hand, to pitch Arnie on why he should put even more capital into Lima One. It was fifty-fifty on how he would respond.

Getting a Lifeline (Top)

Things went so well during my first three months at Lima One that Sandy went ahead with our plan to relocate. After several weekends of house hunting, we were excited to move into a new condo (transformed from an old cotton mill) in downtown Greenville. It had high ceilings and exposed brick, and the neighborhood was safe enough that we could open the windows. We were excited to be reunited in a vibrant new city. But just a few days after our furniture was unloaded and our boxes unpacked, Lima One faced its life-threatening cash crunch.

The same day that JW drove to Atlanta to meet with Arnie, I took Sandy out to a popular pub called the Nose Dive and explained the situation. It didn't go over too well, to put it mildly. "Do you have *any* idea how hard it was for me to pack up the house? Or to find people to rent it, find a new place for us to live, and move the dogs?" I didn't have much of an answer. Her frustration was fully justified.

As our fish-and-chips arrived, there was still no word from JW. I wondered if Arnie would leave us high and dry, and how bad that would be for the company and maybe my marriage as well. Finally, my phone began to vibrate, with JW's name on the screen. "Arnie's good for another two million!" he exclaimed. In my relief I quipped, "If I had known that sooner I would have taken Sandy to Soby's!"—a much nicer restaurant.

This additional investment wasn't a long-term solution, but it would keep us in business while we looked for bigger sources of capital. Over the next year, that search included our botched meeting with William

Erbey in Miami, as well as pitches to various hedge funds, large banks, and money managers in New York. All those pitches were hit-or-miss, mostly miss. We needed a better strategy.

Getting into the Chandelier Bar

Several people advised us to go to the Asset-Backed Security Conference in Las Vegas, a major annual conference for finance professionals, depicted in the book and movie *The Big Short*. We decided that even though it was expensive to attend, we had to give it a shot to connect with institutional investors. Unfortunately, no one told us in advance how the conference actually worked.

Before we left South Carolina, we carefully researched the panel

John Warren and John Thompson at the grand opening of the first Lima One Capital office in Greenville, South Carolina, in 2012.

discussions, debating which ones would be most useful. But when we got to the first panel, there were maybe twenty people in the room. We asked someone why it was so empty, with five thousand finance people at the conference. He explained, "No one comes to Vegas for the panels. They come for wall-to-wall meetings during the day and parties at night." Which meant that by not setting up any meetings in advance, we had already blown it.

Well, maybe not. We got a list of attendees and jumped on LinkedIn to research which ones might be interested in Lima One. Over the next few hours we banged out more than two hundred emails, each personalized with names and details, requesting a meeting at the conference. We spent over $700 in LinkedIn fees to send those targeted messages.

One of those emails impressed a loan trader for Cantor Fitzgerald, Ted Owens. His calendar was already full, of course, but he offered to meet us for a drink with his partner Dan Drew on the final night, at the swanky Chandelier bar in the Cosmopolitan hotel. After we shared our story and plans, Ted and Drew told us that Cantor would represent us as our investment bank. That one drink set the stage for significant investments by two multibillion-dollar hedge funds, which elevated Lima One to a new level. We finally had long-term access to institutional capital and the resources to expand into eighteen additional states, followed eventually by nearly the whole country.

We could have given up when we realized that our original plan for the conference was doomed to fail. But we had been trained as Marines not to quit. Keep digging, try something new, figure it out. Adapt or die.

Making Sense of Our Journey

To fast-forward our story: by 2019 Lima One had expanded into forty-four states, with more than two thousand highly engaged employees offering thousands of customers a wide range of loan products. The company was running like a well-oiled machine and consistently profitable. But precisely because of that success, we felt ready to move on to new challenges. We sold Lima One in a nine-figure deal and completed our transition out by the end of 2020.

Our friends and family assumed that we'd start another business in real estate finance or a related field. Instead, we surprised them by choosing a very different industry that we had to figure out from scratch: cryptocurrency. GEM Mining, also headquartered in Greenville, mines Bitcoin using advanced computers called miners. We raised over $250 million in institutional capital and acquired more than 32,000 miners by the end of 2021. With a tight team of fewer than ten, most of them veterans of Lima One, we're on track to become a significant player in this turbulent new market.

Now that you know the context of our journey from Marines to entrepreneurs, the rest of this book—exploring the nine key strategies of Marine-style leadership—will make a lot more sense. We are 100 percent certain that our successes in Ramadi, at Lima One, and now at GEM Mining are all connected by the consistency of our values and leadership strategies.

When JW launched Lima One, he was simply trying to make a living, but we accidentally ended up proving a point. If the traditional business playbook leans towards short-term thinking, top-down decision making, and treating employees like replaceable cogs in a machine, the Marine Corps playbook is the polar opposite. As you're about to see in detail, the nine key strategies offer a recipe for building a values-driven, inspired, cohesive, resilient, creative, relentless organization—whether its mission is making loans, mining Bitcoin, solving social problems, winning a sports championship, building a nonprofit community, or just about any other field of human endeavor. We're not saying it's easy, but we know this approach works.

If this (admittedly huge) promise sounds appealing, turn the page and let's dig in.

PART II

THE NINE KEY STRATEGIES OF MARINE LEADERSHIP

CHAPTER 3

DO EVERYTHING FOR A REASON

Two Questions after a Deadly Deployment (Top)

About a year and a half before we fought the battle for Ramadi, Lima Company was deployed to another Iraqi city during the Second Battle of Fallujah. That one got much more attention from the media back home, because it was the bloodiest phase of the entire Iraq War. For about six weeks, the Marines saw more killed in action (KIA) in Fallujah than in any conflict since Vietnam. Every street, alleyway, and corner in that deadly city brought a high risk of ambush by insurgent guerrillas, and we simply weren't prepared to counter them. I frequently cursed the fact that we always seemed to be on defense, never on offense.

One person who was equally frustrated by Fallujah was Captain Barela, then serving as Lima Company's forward air controller (FAC), in charge of coordinating all our air support. When Lima Company returned from Fallujah to Camp Lejeune in the fall 2005, he became our company commander. As the company's most senior NCO, I worked closely with Captain Barela to prepare the company for our next deployment back to Iraq. We instantly agreed that our top priority was answering two questions: What went wrong in Fallujah? And what could we do better next time in Ramadi, against an equally relentless insurgency?

The first question had a simple answer: We had gone into Fallujah without any clear strategy to match the circumstances on the ground, which kept us constantly in reaction mode. Dealing with each new crisis immediately in front of us prevented us from devising strategies and tactics to make a serious long-term impact. We were like a football team stuck on defense 90 percent of the time, a path to certain defeat.

The second question—how could we avoid the same problem in Ramadi?—was much tougher. But Max was certain that it had to begin with rethinking everything and insisting on a clear reason for every action. Following traditional combat tactics wouldn't work in this unique environment. We had to go back to the drawing board.

Civilians tend to assume that military strategy is set by generals, not company captains, platoon lieutenants, or gunnery sergeants. But too often in Iraq, the top brass had no idea what was actually happening on the ground. Max concluded that if we wanted a better plan for Ramadi, we would have to devise it ourselves. I didn't realize it at the time, but our discussions at Camp Lejeune were implementing the first and most vital principle we'll cover in this book. We were attacking our problem by doing everything for a reason.

The Most Vital Principle

We put "Do everything for a reason" first on our list of nine key strategies because it was the single most important factor in our effectiveness in Ramadi. Years later, it was bedrock of our success in business. At first glance, this principle sounds simple, if not obvious. How hard can it be to think logically and analyze situations before deciding on strategy and tactics? A lot harder than you may assume.

It's human nature to fall into habits and stick to familiar patterns. Very few people in any field consistently ask, "Why are we doing this?" As one of JW's squad leaders in Ramadi, Corporal Mark Carpenter, told us, "I always thought the best leaders could tell you why you're doing something, not just because they said so." Anyone who gives a "because I said so" response either has a bad reason for doing something or is a poor communicator. Either way, that phrase will kill a team's morale and hurt its long-term success.

Once we learn how to do something and internalize a process, most of us carry it out on autopilot. This pattern is true for both our most inconsequential *and* our most important undertakings. Sticking to habits is a lazy and dangerous way to do things. There's probably a more effective way to do many of the tasks on your plate, especially if you or your organization haven't questioned them in a long time. This is especially true if your culture discourages any challenge to the status quo. We've seen firsthand that in business, doing things without a good reason can be devastating. In combat, it can be deadly.

If doing everything for a reason seems daunting, don't worry. We've developed a five-step process that will help you apply the principle to any challenge you are attacking:

1. Have the right mindset.
2. Conduct a strategic analysis of the battlefield.
3. Set a strategic objective to accomplish.
4. Craft an operational plan to accomplish the overall objective.
5. Develop commonsense tactics and constantly evolve them.

Think Different

The right mindset is essential for anyone attempting to do everything for a reason. You may have to train yourself to keep an open mind about new, untested, and maybe crazy-sounding options. As one of JW's Marines, Corporal Erich Setele, put it, "The best Marines think critically. The most expensive thing a person can own is a closed mind." Do you remember the Apple tagline that Steve Jobs promoted when he returned as CEO in 1997, "Think Different"? It debuted with a commercial called "Here's to the Crazy Ones":

> Here's to the crazy ones. The misfits, the rebels, the troublemakers, the round pegs in the square holes. The ones who see things differently. They're not fond of rules. . . . You can quote them, disagree with them, glorify or vilify them, but the only thing you can't do is ignore them. Because they change things. They push the human race forward. And while some may see them as the crazy ones, we see genius. Because the ones who are crazy enough to think that they can change the world, are the ones who do.

We were fortunate to work for a company commander who was one of those crazy ones. Captain Barela was often willing to break Marine Corps norms to test out new ideas. He also encouraged us to pursue creative solutions to problems. The last thing he wanted was blind obedience to rules. He expected us to combine our training in the Marine Corps way of doing things with our own experience, logic, and common sense. His high expectations empowered and brought out the very best in us.

Like Captain Barela, successful entrepreneurs and other business leaders also tend to think differently. They see a complex problem, analyze it objectively, and look for simple ways to solve it. Then they build a company around that solution. The bigger the problem and the simpler the solution, the more valuable the company.

In contrast, remember Tom, the real estate lending "expert" from the previous chapter? When asked why he made various decisions about underwriting loans, he replied, "This is the way we've always done it." He never learned to think differently from how he had always originated loans. That was literally right after he had gone bankrupt during the financial crisis and was being sued for hundreds of millions of dollars over bad loans. He didn't learn anything from those setbacks, or even seem to want to learn. We took that as a cautionary tale.

Embrace Collaboration

Once a leader is open-minded enough to think differently, he or she must possess enough self-confidence to embrace collaboration. One reason "do everything for a reason" is rarely applied is because too many leaders are insecure. They fear what people will think of them if they don't possess all the answers or provide all the ideas. A leader must accept that he or she doesn't have all the answers. And a leader needs to be willing *not* to be the smartest person in your organization. When a subordinate says, "Hey, what if we tried this idea that nobody's tried before?" you need to subdue your ego. In a healthy culture, it doesn't matter who came up with a new plan. It becomes everyone's plan, and it gets everyone's full support. As Corporal Carpenter put it, "The best leaders don't have to know everything"—and no one expects them to. They do, however, expect leaders to be open-minded enough to listen to additional ideas and facts in order to make the best decision possible.

As we built up our team at Lima One, we stressed "do everything for a reason" as rule #1. On the first day of training for each employee, JW told everyone, "I started this company by myself. Then Top brought different skills and perspectives and took us to a higher level. Since then, each new hire has done the same." We wanted everyone sharing and feeding off each other's ideas. If they had a better way of doing something, we wanted to hear it, and we promised not to get defensive due to ego. As Jim McKeon, one of our lead investors and a key mentor, recalls, "One of the things I really appreciated from both John and Top is they were willing to take other people's experiences, understandings, and capabilities, and allow those to be a part of what ultimately was built into the foundation of the company."

"Do everything for a reason" had the same impact at Lima One as it did in Ramadi. "Lima One was innovative and didn't do things one way because that is how it was always done," says Brandy Cogsdill, our head of loan servicing. People felt empowered to rethink everything, look for new solutions, and share ideas without fear of repercussion. If they didn't understand the reason behind any policy or process, they were expected to take the initiative to find out. Maybe they'd agree with the reason, maybe not, but the extra step of understanding was essential.

No one ever got in trouble for making a suggestion, even a bad one. But they could get in serious trouble if they couldn't explain why they were doing something related to their job. And if they were ever dumb enough to answer, "Because we've always done it this way"—that was a firing offense.

We even took advantage of opportunities to collaborate with and learn from groups outside of our company. "We had enough humility to recognize that there might be best practices that we could glean from others," recalls Chief Financial Officer Josh Woodward. "We often asked, 'What are some things that we're not doing that you think we should be doing?'—specifically to banks and investors when they would come in or when we would visit and pitch our business."

The Strategic Analysis of the Insurgency

Captain Barela didn't blindly trust any strategies set by the top brass; he needed to confirm that they really made sense. In preparing for our Ramadi deployment, he conducted a strategic analysis of the upcoming battlefield. He went beyond what had happened during our Fallujah deployment to ask an even more fundamental question: Why was there an insurgency in Iraq at all?

Few strategic planners in the Pentagon or the government even bothered to ask this question, and we doubt any other company commander was asking it. Most of them were just trying to find and neutralize the bad guys who kept laying IEDs and shooting RPGs. These planners failed to think strategically. They were good at reacting to what was happening on the surface but never got to the root problem. It was the equivalent of a doctor repeatedly giving a patient pain medication for an arm that was hurting, but never doing an X-ray to see that the arm was broken and needed a cast to heal.

Captain Barela analyzed the insurgency with fresh eyes and no preconceived notions. He studied the history of insurgencies from the Roman Empire through the Vietnam War, in search of parallels that might help us. "When I was a lieutenant, I started heavily reading counterinsurgency books because that is the way I did battle study," Captain Barela recalls. "I would find three books on a battle from hopefully different perspectives, and then I would read all three to get something different from each author."

He concluded, and we later confirmed in-country, that the root cause of the Iraqi insurgency was "de-Baathification." This flawed American policy was created and mandated by the occupation administrator Paul Bremer after the initial invasion of Iraq in 2003 ousted Saddam Hussein from power. It barred former members of Saddam Hussein's ruling Baath Party from serving in the new Iraqi government and disbanded the Iraqi Army.

Bremer incorrectly assumed that virtually all Sunni Muslims in Iraq were supporters of al-Qaeda because they were Baath Party members like Hussein. It proved to be a disastrous mistake by a reckless civilian appointee who had no understanding of Iraqi history or the Shia-Sunni conflict. "De-Baathification" disenfranchised one-third of the population, including the country's most competent leaders. It also left a half million heavily armed men unemployed, disgruntled, and free to roam the streets.

Prior to April 4, 2004, there had been no Marines killed in Ramadi, and very few casualties. This suddenly changed when Second Battalion, Fourth Marines lost twelve troops over a three-day period. Armed mobs were now roving around Anbar Province, organizing into more than twenty different insurgent groups. Because of a lack of security throughout the country, foreign terrorists were also flooding into Iraq to wage jihad, including cells from al-Qaeda and at least a few Chechen snipers.

Despite the huge range of these insurgent groups, they could be sorted into two main categories: al-Qaeda and its supporters versus Iraqi Sunni nationalists. The difference between those groups—a difference previously ignored by most American forces—would be the key to restoring peace.

Al-Qaeda in Iraq, led by Abu Musab al-Zarqawi, was truly evil, like the al-Qaeda cells that had carried out the attacks of September 11, 2001. They were religious frauds, pretending to be devoted to Islam while deploying ruthless mafia tactics to gain power and money. They ignored every Islamic rule and ethical principle, including prohibitions against drinking alcohol, killing children, raping women, and torturing prisoners. There was no hope of negotiating with al-Qaeda. We had to either kill or capture them because they wouldn't hesitate to kill us.

The other broad category of Sunni insurgents, whom we called the nationalists, were much more numerous. The leaders of the nationalists included former Iraqi Army officers, tribal leaders, sheikhs, and imams. They viewed the Shia-governed Iran as their long-standing enemy. The nationalists also viewed the United States as an enemy, because it was occupying their country. But they also hated al-Qaeda for all the death and destruction it was causing. Above all, the nationalists wanted the violence and chaos to stop, so they could try to rebuild normal lives.

This was the strategic situation in Iraq that almost everyone in a position of power in the United States previously missed, including the military. Luckily, Captain Barela conducted an objective and thorough analysis of the roots of the insurgency. Next, he needed to set our strategic objective and come up with a plan for accomplishing it.

Set a Strategic Objective

Once Captain Barela understood the roots of the insurgency and distinguished the two types of insurgents, he decided that the nationalists could be reasoned with and incentivized, because they had understandable demands and a basic respect for human life. If true, this would give us a huge opportunity. If we played our cards right, we could partner with the nationalists against al-Qaeda by convincing them that the Marines truly wanted to restore peace and a normal life in Ramadi. The nationalists might then be willing to provide us with the necessary human intelligence to wreak havoc on al-Qaeda.

Based on this reasoning, Captain Barela set our strategic objective: to co-opt the local population and nationalist leaders in order to disrupt al-Qaeda. This objective was clear and achievable. Every Marine in our company understood it and worked towards achieving it.

Years later at Lima One, we called our strategic objective our "company mission." It also became our tagline: "Lima One Capital, the nation's premier lender for residential real estate investors." Although short, it implied many different things that we could convey to our employees, investors, and customers. "The nation's" conveyed a national, geographic footprint. "Premier" conveyed "best in class," but not necessarily the largest. It implied quality loans and quality customer service. And "lender for residential real estate investors" suggested our laser-focused objective. The company's mission statement proved to be a resounding success.

Any organization's strategic objective should be inspirational and aspirational. It should be lofty but achievable. It should be a goal the team will rally around and do everything in their power to achieve.

Crafting the Operational Plan for Ramadi

Now that Lima Company had a strategic objective—partnering with the local population and nationalist leaders to disrupt al-Qaeda—we needed to craft a detailed operational plan to achieve it. This plan would include our training for the deployment and our key initiatives that we would attempt once we arrived in Ramadi.

Top and Captain Barela drew on their experiences in Fallujah to devise a new training plan for the company. Before we left the United States again, our Marines needed to be well trained in patrolling, communicating, and setting up firing positions against an ever-shifting insurgency. They also needed to be using live ammunition under simulated battle conditions.

Once we got to Ramadi, we would have to overcome two huge challenges. First, we needed to win over the local population, as discussed above. Second, we needed to develop actionable intelligence in order to capture or kill al-Qaeda fighters in our sector. Captain Barela devised an innovative plan that would bring us closer to both goals at the same time. Lima Company would conduct a literal census of every military-aged male (ages fifteen and up) in our area of operations. If we really wanted to know the local civilians, develop relationships, and win their help to gather vital intelligence, it had to be done one conversation at a time.

This meant that Marines would need to visit thousands of houses, via constant and continuous foot patrols all over our sector. We met civilians face-to-face, instead of just driving around in our Humvees. When a squad of Marines (plus an interpreter) visited a house, we were always very respectful. We stayed away from the women and didn't speak with them unless they interacted with us first. We tried to establish common ground by discussing our own families. The kids would look at us as if we were aliens from outer space, with our seventy-five to one hundred pounds of gear, M16s, and night-vision goggles. But if their parents allowed, we gave them candy or a soccer ball to show goodwill.

Then we looked the men in the eye and had a very candid conversation. We began every meeting by telling them, "We are a new Marine unit here in Ramadi. Our goals are to protect you and your family, and to kill or capture al-Qaeda." For most people in Ramadi, if they had previously interacted with Marines, they had already heard that line. But they had not heard our next line: "If you are a nationalist who has taken up arms against previous American troops, we forgive you for all of your previous sins. In exchange, we ask that you forgive us for any previous sins against you."

We continued by explaining our shared goals for their city and

First Platoon squad leader Sergeant Marco Cruz handing out school supplies to local Iraqi children in Ramadi, Iraq.

country and made clear that they knew that al-Qaeda was fighting for the opposite of those goals. We also told them that we would do our best to repair the local infrastructure. We tried to get sewer systems and water systems repaired. At one point we brought in fifteen hundred generators that we gave to local families that didn't have electricity.

We then respectfully asked for their help. Did they know anyone involved with al-Qaeda? Could they help us get meetings with tribal leaders in their neighborhood? Would they be willing to contact us if they heard about an attack being planned? We promised that we would do everything in our power to protect them if they gave us information that would help us drive al-Qaeda away.

We received minimal help or cooperation for the first couple of months. Little by little, however, we began to win the trust and respect of the local nationalists and ordinary civilians. Many of them risked deadly reprisals to help us find and neutralize al-Qaeda. After six to eight weeks of foot patrols for our census, we had enough information to compile a huge database of almost every house and civilian in the sector. That census became our key tool in the hunt for al-Qaeda cells.

Corporal Daniel Tarantino, a squad leader for Fourth Platoon, recalls a conversation he had with a local man in Ramadi: "He asked me, 'Why is it that you all treat us the way you do? More kindly than the other Marines that have been here?' And I just said the first thing that came to my mind: 'I am treating you guys the way I would want you to treat us if Iraqis ever came to America.' And it brought him to tears. I remember it being one of the more powerful exchanges I had with one of the locals. And I had that kind of conversation on more than one occasion." With repeated interactions like that one, we began to make deep inroads with the population.

By the third month of the deployment, we had trusted sources throughout Ramadi who were providing actionable intelligence. They served us chai tea at night in their homes, an Iraqi tradition of hospitality that reminded us of sweet tea from the American South; that tea helped bridge the cultural gap. A few nights later we'd use the information they gave us to conduct raids on terrorist cells. Our plan to rid Ramadi of al-Qaeda was working.

Captain Barela did an amazing job developing our initial operational plan. The platoon commanders and company staff then expanded that plan and eventually perfected our tactics. It was a perfect example of doing everything for a reason, and of how the power of collaboration further strengthens great leaders and great plans.

Tactical-Level Execution

As important as it is to ask, "Why are we doing this?" about big strategic questions, it's equally important to ask it about tactics. Sometimes it's seemingly minor tactical decisions that make all the difference. Sometimes you must abandon standard practice or even break the rules of your organization. For example, Marine doctrine said that if you were guarding a building, you should put four riflemen on the corners of the roof. But in Ramadi, where we might face deadly Chechen snipers at any moment, that was crazy. We unilaterally switched to putting our riflemen inside the top floor of a building, looking out of windows using mirrors.

Another crucial example was our response to taking fire from terrorists hiding in a particular house. The battalion before us would often call for air strikes to take out a house full of insurgents, but their approach failed to weigh the pros and cons of dropping bombs. Applying common sense showed that air strikes did much more harm than good. The United States has incredible airpower, but in a densely populated area, there was a good chance that a bomb dropped from twenty thousand feet might be a few feet off target, destroying the homes of innocent neighbors. And if American forces accidentally killed, injured, or destroyed the property of the innocent, word would spread quickly and destroy our goodwill among the population. Al-Qaeda would use bombing mistakes as a recruiting tool.

So Lima Company eliminated air strikes in our sector. Whenever we took fire from insurgents inside a house or building, we went in with Marines on foot, cleared the house, and took out the insurgents. Once the population saw that we were serious about ending air strikes, they began to trust us more.

The same was true for bending Marine procedures around foot patrols. Although higher-ups had put a requirement in place to have a minimum of six Marines together at all times, we disregarded that rule because it endangered our intelligence sources. If six Marines showed up at the home of a cooperative nationalist, that would be painting a bull's-eye on his family for al-Qaeda. The new protocol we came up with had a group of just three (often JW, a radio operator, and a translator) talking quietly to our source at night, while other teams of Marines visited every other house on that street, just making friendly conversation. The next morning, when al-Qaeda came around to ask who had been talking to the Americans, the answer was everyone. Our source was protected because the terrorists couldn't kill the entire neighborhood. We were proud that not a single Iraqi collaborator who gave us intel was identified and killed by al-Qaeda during our deployment.

We even created a commonsense approach for when we occupied a house for a day or two for observation. We paid the family twenty dollars a night for their inconvenience. During those temporary house occupations, we let family members come and go as they pleased, except for one who always had to stay in the house with the Marine squad. That person became our insurance policy, so that no one else in the family would have a change of heart and betray our position to al-Qaeda. Any RPG that took out the Marines would kill their loved one, too.

Facing Organizational Resistance

One downside of doing everything for a reason is that you will inevitably encounter resistance from people who *don't* do everything for a reason— either because they're afraid to challenge the status quo or because they can't think logically and independently. Some people become jealous or defensive when witnessing the successful results that come from this principle.

In Ramadi, some Marines within our battalion questioned our foot patrols and census. Some even tried to shame us by calling us sissies or "muj lovers," short for *mujahideen*. They'd say things like "Real Marines are killers, not census takers. You guys should go work for the Census Bureau!" It was a very narrow mindset, opposed to innovation. Yes, Marines can be killers when necessary, and Lima Company killed more than our share of jihadists. But we weren't *only* killers, because this mission required more than brute force.

It was bad enough that we got grief from our peers, but we also got it from our own battalion commander. Because he rarely visited his four infantry companies stationed throughout the city, he never saw what we were doing up close. As a result, he had no idea what was really going on in our sector or the progress we were making towards defeating the insurgency. Our battalion commander had disdain for Captain Barela because he applied "do everything for a reason" to every aspect of our deployment, and because he was openly defiant when carrying out his innovations. But none of our initial critics could ignore our results. The longer our deployment lasted, the more our sector stabilized, and the fewer attacks we faced.

By July 2006, conditions had improved to the point that we could turn over Snakepit to the Iraqi Security Force (ISF) and the Iraqi police, while we occupied OPVA full-time. The ISF took over patrols in its own sector of western Ramadi—the first battle space independently operated by the ISF anywhere in the dangerous Anbar Province. Lima Company was also given an additional area of operations to patrol, bigger than the territory we gave up to ISF. By the time our deployment ended that October, violent attacks by insurgents were down by at least 50 percent since our arrival that March. We had also captured the leader of al-Qaeda in Ramadi, Bakr Muhammad Halice.

As word got around about our methods, other leaders came to observe us. One was Lieutenant Colonel William Jurney (now a three-star general), the battalion commander of First Battalion, Sixth Marines, which would soon replace our battalion in Ramadi. He patrolled nonstop with us for several days and talked to all the Marines in our company to get different accounts of the current situation in Ramadi. Then he ordered his battalion to apply our foot patrolling and census tactics across the board. Jurney exemplified a great battalion commander.

About six months after Lima Company's departure, the violence had subsided so much that First Battalion, Sixth Marines could walk around Ramadi without flak jackets. And about a year after our departure, they staged a fun run through the streets of Ramadi to celebrate the Marine Corps' birthday. The difference was that dramatic. We were especially pleased that after our deployment, Captain Barela and Top were asked to contribute to the writing of the official Marine Infantry Company Operations Manual. Their sections focused on counterinsurgency operations at the company level.

"What Isn't Here That Should Be Here?" (JW)

We faced similar resistance for similar reasons as we built Lima One Capital. People questioned almost everything about our way of doing things. We heard dismissive comments like, "You can't build a finance company in South Carolina. . . . Your hiring practices are not normal. . . . Your processes haven't been tried before." As our director of operations, Rankin Blair, recalls, "It was common for investors to dismiss our processes or even outright laugh at how we approached certain problems. However, over time these same people ended up adopting or complementing these same processes."

People criticize whatever they don't understand if it breaks traditions or norms. But when something starts working, they can't argue with success. So when you do everything for a reason and encounter stiff resistance, keep pushing forward. Even your toughest critics may eventually come around. (And if they don't, who cares!)

When I founded Lima One I had friends working at three major banks who got me copies of their lending guidelines. Three huge volumes filled with rules about commercial, residential, and construction loans. I started going through them with objectivity, thinking like an outsider. "Why is this rule here?" If it didn't make any sense, I took it out. When I was done, 75 percent of those fat volumes were crossed out, and we kept the best of each. (To be fair, some of what we cut was due to banking regulations that didn't apply to Lima One.)

Then I asked, "What isn't here that should be here?" That question led to some new guidelines that others weren't using, such as providing loans based on the future value of the property after repairs and renovations were completed, not the current value. We also set goals of increasing the speed of our loan closings. Just because a bank took thirty to forty-five days to close didn't mean we needed to follow suit. As a result, Lima One closed virtually all loans within ten days, giving us a huge competitive advantage.

We even created new loan products differently. About 99 percent of lenders start by asking what kinds of loans the capital markets will invest in. Then they offer those loan formats to their customers, take it or leave it. But we worked the opposite way, designing our loans to fit the needs of our customers. Although our loans looked different at first glance, we were able to convince institutional investors to finance them because they were paid off at exceptionally high rates, with less than 1 percent of them ending in foreclosure. That changed the game in our industry, just as counterinsurgency did in Ramadi.

The Process Never Ends

Counterinsurgency prepared us well for business because the situation in Ramadi was constantly changing. We would come up with new tactics and make progress, but then the insurgents would adapt and try something new. We could never afford to get complacent or think we had every possibility covered. We constantly had to analyze and reanalyze. Why are we doing this? Does it still make sense? Is there a better way?

Great leaders in any field do that kind of rethinking whenever circumstances change. Think of a football coach who is losing at halftime, or an investor whose trading strategy is getting crushed by the market. You need the discipline to stay open-minded, and it's not easy to build up that kind of discipline.

It's also not easy to set aside your emotions and your ego so they won't cloud your judgment. In Iraq we couldn't allow our overall strategy to be thrown off by specific bad outcomes. For instance, if a Marine was killed by an IED during a foot patrol, that was a tragedy, but it didn't mean we were wrong to be doing foot patrols. We always had to weigh the risks against the benefits, using logic rather than emotion.

Business can get very emotional, too. Today we look at the value of

Bitcoin fluctuating daily, sometimes looking like the EKG readings of a patient having a heart attack. On any day when Bitcoin has a steep drop, it would be easy to panic and make an impulsive strategic shift. Instead, we tune out the day-to-day noise and focus on our long-term mission. We're prepared to pivot if necessary, but we're not going to be driven into any impulsive changes.

It can be a fine line sometimes between rationally staying the course and irrationally resisting change, but it's essential to stay on the right side of that line. Ask questions, apply logic, test new ideas, evaluate them without ego, and encourage all your people to do the same. Doing everything for a reason can become the bedrock for your future success.

CHAPTER 4

BUILD A TEAM
OF KILLERS

The Case for Hiring Bartenders (Top)

As a proud Irish American, I like to throw a party at my house every St. Patrick's Day. In 2013, I moved that party to Greenville for the first time, and I hired a local bartending company to set up in my backyard. They sent a young bartender named Stacy Woods. Just by watching her get organized for the event, I could tell that she was attentive to detail. And by watching her juggle the many complicated drink orders of my guests, I could tell that she was smart, calm under pressure, and great with people.

As the party wound down, I pulled Stacy aside and asked how she got into this kind of work. She said, "I just graduated from college a few months ago. I worked my way through college on my own, with three part-time jobs at a time. Right now I'm in a transition phase, trying to figure out my next move. I thought bartending would give me some opportunities to network with businesspeople."

She clearly had grit, a strong work ethic, and something to prove. She seemed humble and personable, too. I told Stacy, "Tomorrow, first thing, please email me your resume." Then I went to find JW at the party. "Did you notice the bartender? She's extremely impressive. Tomorrow I'm getting her resume." He understood immediately, and less than a week later, after interviews and reference checks, we offered Stacy a job. She rose steadily over the next few years and eventually led our short-term finance team, a critical role at Lima One.

When Stacy got married in 2014, she had the reception at a local venue in Greenville called the Cigar Warehouse, and she hired her friends from the same bartending company where she previously worked. This time the main bartender was a young man named Dustin Simmons. Since Stacy had become a vital part of our team, we thought her fellow bartender might also be worth getting to know. JW and I chatted with Dustin while he poured drinks. He turned out to be a Marine veteran, the crew chief of an amphibious assault vehicle. He was wounded in combat, with both of his eardrums blown out from an IED strike, which earned him a Purple Heart.

After Dustin got out of the Marines, he took some manufacturing jobs in his hometown of Greenville, while also bartending nights and weekends. He said he was in a tough situation as a single parent of a young daughter. He needed to earn as much as possible to support his daughter, and he was looking for a new career with a shot at upward mobility.

"It was a group that I wanted to be a part of," Dustin remembers of the Lima One guests at Stacy's wedding. "The employees acted like a family; I could tell that. They enjoyed having a good time, but they were determined. I wanted to surround myself with those like-minded people."

I immediately thought Dustin was really sharp and likable, and I was impressed with how he was handling his personal challenges. It also didn't hurt that he knew how to pour a stiff drink for his fellow Marines! We invited him in for interviews. He didn't have a college degree, and he knew absolutely nothing about finance or real estate. But he passed our values checklist with flying colors. We could tell that he had the character, passion, and work ethic to succeed as an underwriter, just as he had thrived at his manufacturing and bartending jobs.

Initially, Dustin wondered if he was the right fit for a finance company. "I was very hesitant because finance was not my background," he says. "The Marine Corps, construction, and production management were my core work experience. But Lima One took someone who didn't have a background in finance or real estate, and took the time to teach me the industry."

Dustin worked hard, mastered his new role, and got promoted to senior analyst. Eventually he earned another promotion to supervise the short-term financing group. By then he was leading an important team, making a significant amount of money, and supporting his daughter with the quality of life he wanted for her. Dustin is still at Lima One and currently holds the position of operations training and implementation manager.

Hiring is too important to be left to the obsolete standards and practices of traditional human resources (HR) departments. We believe that the current epidemic of job hopping and turnover, the so-called Great Resignation, is at least partly due to mismatches during the recruiting process. Companies and other organizations invest a lot of time and resources in hiring and training people, only to lose too many of them within the first twelve to eighteen months. Each time someone quits, companies have to restart the hiring and training process from scratch. That wasted time holds back the performance of too many organizations.

We've found that it's fairly easy to teach technical skills to someone like Dustin who doesn't have relevant experience. But it's hard if not impossible to teach values and character. Dustin sums up our philosophy best: "I've seen over the past seven years that the most success we've had in hiring is when we take people who understand those values with no experience, and train them ourselves. We plant that seed and watch it grow."

Our hiring practices were abnormal for business, but we knew from day one that they would work, because they came straight from the Marines.

What's a Team of Killers? (JW)

When people ask me to sum up the essence of the Marine Corps, I urge them to watch the first few minutes of a decade-old PBS documentary called simply *The Marines.** It does a masterful job of gathering insights by a range of Marine veterans, historians, and journalists. Some of their comments:

> Marines are different. . . . Their culture is a warrior spirit.
>
> We do the kind of things that our country would ask of its elite warriors.
>
> The Marines run to the sound of the guns.
>
> They're a cult that works. They're a gang that's lawful.
>
> It's the baddest fraternity on the planet.
>
> The professional warrior has a very strong emphasis on a code of ethics. Integrity, morality is a big factor.
>
> A Marine, no matter how many times you knock him down, is going to get to his feet. And that probably makes us as feared as any organization in the world.

Civilians might be put off by some of this strong language. *Warrior? Cult? Gang?* But those are mostly metaphors, as is another Marine phrase: *team of killers.* Yes, sometimes Marines have to kill, but "team of killers" really means killer performance, killer focus, killer clarity of purpose,

---

*   *The Marines*, PBS, aired on August 29, 2006, https://www.pbs.org/video/the-marines-9obwwv/.

killer commitment to the mission, and killer loyalty to each other. Most civilian leaders would do anything to be able to build that kind of team. But too often they get tripped up by dysfunctional processes for hiring, training, and evaluating their people.

This chapter will show you what we learned from the Marines about building teams full of passionately committed people. Then Chapter 5 will focus on how to train your people for maximum effectiveness and evaluate their performance. In other words, first hire your team of killers, then train them. Between these two chapters, you'll see how we applied the best aspects of Marine Corps recruiting and training as we scaled Lima One to become a high-performing force of more than two hundred.*

One reason we were so confident about Marine-style hiring is that it was the first aspect of the Corps that we both experienced, back when we were both trying to become Marines. And those experiences were especially memorable for us both.

Offended and Pissed-off (Top)

On a spring evening in 1989, I was an offended, pissed-off high school senior. On the kitchen table of our Long Island home were acceptance letters from two good state universities. But instead of helping me choose between them, my dad had just told me he wasn't going to pay for either one. Instead, he wanted me to go to a local community college. "It's just for a year or two. You can live at home."

But I didn't want to keep living at home—I wanted to see the world, or at least another part of New York State. When I asked why he was being so tough, Dad admitted that he didn't think I could handle a

---

* We won't say much about GEM Mining in these two chapters because most of our people are former Lima One employees. We already knew they were great when we hired them! And our new CFO is a Marine.

four-year university. He thought I was unfocused and undisciplined. If I did well at community college, he added, he'd be willing to pay for a transfer to a university later. In my frustration, I told him no thanks, I'll find another way to get out of town.

I recalled how my uncles and grandfathers, all veterans, always spoke highly of the Marines. I also had a friend named Jack, a couple of years older, who had joined the Corps right after high school. Prior to enlisting, he was in average shape and somewhat lazy. But when he came home on leave, he was in great shape and radiated self-confidence. He told me joining the Marines was the best decision he'd ever made.

When I went to a Marine recruiting office, I figured I'd just have to fill out some papers. But first, a recruiter grilled me about why I wanted to enlist. What made me think I had the potential to be a Marine? Why should they take a chance on me? His questions were much tougher than I expected, but I guess I did well enough because they sent me home with a permission form. I was young for my grade and would still be seventeen at graduation, so I needed the consent of both parents to enlist.

My mom signed the form immediately, maybe just to get me out of the house. But the guy who said I wasn't disciplined enough for a university was reluctant to let me join the Marines. That made no sense—where else did he think I'd have a better opportunity to develop discipline? Looking back, I think my dad was waiting to see if I'd have a change of heart. He didn't want me to make a knee-jerk decision to spite him. Eventually, he gave in and signed.

My commitment to the Marines was for four years. I assumed I'd get out at twenty-one, then use the GI Bill to pay for college and start a career. It never even occurred to me that I might stay for the next two decades, but at each decision point going forward I saw no reason to leave. Not long after boot camp at Parris Island, Saddam Hussein invaded Kuwait, which led to my first combat deployment during Operation Desert Shield and then Desert Storm. Over the next twenty years I served several more overseas deployments, including in Kosovo, Haiti, and Fallujah, while moving up the NCO ranks to master sergeant. I guess that Long Island recruiter made a pretty good call to let me in.

My Generation's Time to Step Up (JW)

I grew up in a very patriotic family in South Carolina. Almost every Sunday afternoon during the fall and winter, we watched a classic military movie like *Sands of Iwo Jima*. Both of my grandfathers had served in World War II, and I idolized them. Nevertheless, I had no interest in joining the military. Even though I was recruited by both the US Military Academy and the US Naval Academy to play basketball, I chose to go to Washington and Lee University, in Lexington, Virginia. I didn't even take advantage of its ROTC programs. My dad later joked, "If you had figured out your goals just a few years earlier, you could have saved me lot of money in tuition."

My attitude started to change when I did a summer internship in Washington, DC, with Representative Floyd Spence, the chairman of the House Armed Services Committee. His chief of staff, Craig Metz, made a concerted effort to expose me to all branches of the military, and I became especially impressed with the Marines. My admiration grew as we watched a parade honoring Korean War veterans on that war's fiftieth anniversary. The Marines stood out as fundamentally different from the other branches.

On September 11, 2001, I was a junior in college and learned of the attacks shortly after leaving my 8:30 a.m. class on classical political thought. I stayed glued to the TV all day and late into the night. I was angry at al-Qaeda and anyone who claimed their attacks were justified. I felt like it was my generation's time to step up and defend the country during a crisis, just as our fathers and grandfathers had done. Soon after 9/11, I wrote a term paper on how the working class did a disproportionate share of the fighting and dying in Vietnam, while the sons of the elite avoided the draft. I quoted *Fields of Fire* by James Webb: "Who are the young men that we are asking to go into action against such solid odds? They are the best we have. But they are not McNamara's sons, or Bundy's. . . . And they know they're at the end of the pipeline. That no one cares. They know." I realized that I'd be a hypocrite if I left it to less privileged Americans to fight the War on Terror.

I later wrote an honors thesis about my grandfather's B-24 bomber squadron in the Pacific during World War II. I interviewed thirty of those veterans, and almost all said variations of the same line: "I wasn't a hero. I was just doing my duty." That quote penetrated my heart. I wanted to serve, not for personal glory but because it was the right thing to do. I applied to Marine Officer Candidates School, aiming to start in the summer of 2003, right after my college graduation.

When the United States invaded Iraq that March, I worried that the war would be over before I could get there. I was even more frustrated when the Marines said they had no open slots for OCS until January 2004. But a month later, the recruiter called back to say an OCS slot had suddenly opened. All I had to do was pass the physical fitness test, which I assumed would be easy since I was in good shape. But I failed it—couldn't do enough pull-ups. From that day forward, I resolved to be ready whenever another OCS slot opened. After graduation I took a management-track job with Michelin, and all I did in my spare time was train hard. I got into much better shape, and when I finally got a chance to retake the PFT, I earned a perfect score.

Many friends and family thought I was crazy, either because I might be killed or because they thought the military was beneath me. "Why throw away your education? You don't need to do this." But I did need to do it. As I wrote in my journal just before going to Iraq, if I'd chosen another path, "No matter how much money I made, or what position I held, there would always be a haunting question deep down in my soul. . . . I wanted to know and had to know what I was made of. Maybe no one else would have questioned it, but I would have and that's enough."

Start with Core Values

Like the Marines, Lima One hired candidates based on their core values and core competencies, knowing that we could train them later for specific job skills. That was our fundamental principle in building amazing teams. "It was pivotal to our success," recalls Josh Woodward, employee number six and our eventual CFO. "It allowed us to attract amazing people who fit our culture exceptionally well. Once these individuals were given a chance and were successful, both as a result of their innate values and competencies and as a result of the culture itself, they were immensely loyal and attracted other amazingly high-quality people. Even when these people lacked experience, our emphasis on training supported them and created conditions for their success."

In contrast, many companies struggle to hire and retain great people because they don't think about what's most important when hiring. They focus on relevant degrees and industry experience, often ignoring the core values of potential new hires during the screening process. If you ask the leaders of these companies how they chose their hiring criteria, they usually say something like, "It's an industry standard. Besides, we've always done it this way." They ignore the first principle of doing everything for a reason.

For instance, more jobs than ever require a college degree, even though the actual work doesn't require anything that someone might learn in college. Don't get us wrong—the majority of our hires at Lima One were college grads who turned out to be top-notch performers. But we also know that a diploma isn't the only way to prove someone's intelligence or discipline. Plenty of smart, enthusiastic, hardworking people don't go to college for one reason or another, and it seems crazy to automatically exclude them from your hiring process. Top, who bypassed college for a different and more dangerous challenge, is a prime example.

The same applies to snobbery about where people went to college. "Lima One's hiring practices were definitely unique," says Jim McKeon. "You didn't have to go to Harvard or Princeton or Stanford. We recruited character and attitude. And the presumption was, if they had character and attitude and especially a military background, competence comes along with that." What matters isn't how prestigious someone's school is, but how much that candidate has done with whatever opportunities were available to them.

The Marines don't recruit people with combat experience; they look for people with the values, aptitudes, and commitment necessary to thrive in combat. Judging people by their potential, not their pedigree, is the key to the meritocracy of the Corps. It's relatively easy to teach a young recruit the physical skills of operating weapons and other equipment, but it's extremely hard if not impossible to teach the character traits that keep a Marine focused and calm under fire, and willing to run towards the sound of gunfire instead of in the opposite direction.

In analyzing the most common traits of Marines, we found that most share five essential values:

- Grit—the determination to keep going in the face of adversity
- Honesty—the character and integrity to own up to mistakes and face consequences, rather than deflecting blame
- Work ethic—the deep belief that any worthwhile outcome requires hard, sustained work, and you can never expect something for nothing
- Team spirit—the willingness to put the needs of the collective ahead of the needs or desires of the individual
- Something to prove—the need to show critics and doubters (personal or professional) that they underestimated you

These are the dominating traits of "killers" in the civilian world as well. And they usually overlap. People with something to prove tend to be willing to work the hardest to prove it, and they usually display grit when things get exceptionally hard. You should rush to hire people who display all five values, regardless of whatever education or experience they have on their resumes. These are the men and women you want in your foxhole. You can screen for them by focusing on the criteria that really matter:

- Do their words and actions demonstrate honesty and integrity?
- Have they displayed a strong work ethic, grit, and poise under adversity?
- Are they clearly willing to commit to a mission bigger than their own self-interest?
- Are they determined to prove themselves to their family, friends, peers, or the world?

The Walk-on: Cortney

We started putting these ideas into practice when we hired the first Lima One employee other than our administrative assistant—our fourth person overall. We were growing quickly and desperately needed a sales rep to network at industry events and find new clients. When we posted the job listing, we were concerned about getting good applicants, since we were still so small and new. One resume came from Cortney Newmans, a football player who had recently graduated from the University of Georgia.

"I had started working at State Farm, trying to build my own book of business," recalls Cortney. "I reached out when that role became available because I felt like I had a greater purpose. I also had a love for real estate." Top interviewed Cortney first and liked him immediately. He had no experience in finance, real estate, or sales, but his character and values were outstanding. Cortney had lost his mom at age eight and was raised by his father, an African American Baptist minister in Macon, Georgia. His dad sacrificed a lot to send him to a Catholic school so he could get a great education.

Cortney earned an academic scholarship to UGA and made the football team as a walk-on fullback. By his junior year, he had earned a full scholarship for football. It's an amazing story of hard work and grit. But his dad, tragically, didn't get to see him graduate, dying suddenly during Cortney's junior year. After that his closest relative was his be-loved grandmother. He drove home from Athens, Georgia, to Macon nearly every weekend to visit her—a tradition he continued after he joined us in Greenville, requiring a much longer drive.

We were both super impressed by Cortney's character, work ethic, and grit. He was also extremely personable, friendly, and empathetic. We weren't deterred at all by his lack of specific experience. And just as we hoped, he became a perfect example for how fast we could train a qualified hire to become a Lima One sales rep. He started killing it within a few weeks, creating an immediate impact on our business. To this day, he is probably the highest-paid Lima One employee, accounting for more loan originations than any other rep at the company. There is no employee whom we are prouder of than Cortney—and he's equally grateful:

> It really showed me a lot when you took a chance on a young black man who was just twenty-two, just out of college, to run the Atlanta market. In the back of my mind for the eight years that we were to-gether, I thought, *Hey, I'm not going to let them down. I'm going to work as hard as I can to make sure this is a success for everyone across the board.* I knew that you would teach me the business. And then it was up to me to be able to blossom it from there, which it did. I was very grateful that you guys gave chances to people who didn't have experience.

Adding Core Competencies on Top of Core Values

As with core values, it's possible to gauge someone's core competen-cies without the traditional corporate obsession with credentials and industry experience. That obsession never made any sense to us. Why should we hire an underwriter with twenty years' experience who changed jobs every eighteen months? We actually felt that prior expe-rience in real estate or lending was more of a negative than a positive. Someone who worked at a conventional financial institution would

John Warren and Cortney Newmans at a real estate investment club meeting in Atlanta, Georgia, in October 2012.

have absorbed practices that Lima One rejected, which meant they'd have a lot to *unlearn* along with a lot to learn.

Instead, we set out to judge core competencies based on the skills people demonstrated, no matter where or how they had honed them. For instance, what did it take to be a successful underwriter? It mostly required the ability to communicate clearly, listen attentively, manage expectations, and evaluate credibility and trustworthiness. An underwriter also needed to be able to multitask, pay attention to details, and hit tight deadlines. You could learn those skills through lots of different experiences, in both academia and the real world. We looked for ways to measure what people could actually accomplish if we gave them a shot.

We started to interview people about their entire lives, not just their past jobs and education. Some personal questions—maybe too personal by the standards of a corporate HR department—could be extremely revealing. We asked about their upbringing, their hobbies, their passions outside of work. We asked what they *really* wanted for their careers and their lives, other than a paycheck. We asked who they truly cared about. We found that once we established a conversational rapport, people would usually reveal their true personalities, instead of giving canned answers to the typical, boring interview questions. And they would show us what they were really good at.

If applicants could clear the hurdles of both core values and core competencies, we'd be happy to teach them the technical aspects of our business. If they couldn't, we would turn them away, no matter how strong their resumes or how desperate we were to fill a role. The result was that we started to fill our ranks not merely with excellent employees, but with extremely *loyal* employees who appreciated their opportunities. "This philosophy helped us foster a very strong culture and ensured that many of the earliest employees bought into the mission," recalls Justin Thompson, who was employee number five and our marketing director.

We heard something similar from Katie Summersett, employee number seven, whom we hired straight out of Clemson University with no directly applicable experience. "If this philosophy didn't exist, I wouldn't be where I am today. It's one of the main contributing factors of Lima One's success." Drew Fitzpatrick, one of our longtime directors, agreed. "This philosophy is one of the single greatest components of John and Top's leadership and one that employees at Lima One were most grateful for. Their ability to look beyond direct experience and to recognize talent is uncommon in any industry."

Initially, we faced a lot of pushback about our hiring methods from potential investors and service providers. Jim McKeon remembers some of the flak we took during the Q&A portions of our early pitch meetings:

In a meeting at Credit Suisse, someone said, "Hey, your underwriters don't have any banking experience." [JW's] response was, "Why would they? Look at what happened to cause the financial crisis. Look what happened to this world the last three or four years. They contributed to that. That's the way it used to be done." That was a bold answer to a bunch of bankers who thought their hiring practices were best. But it was right. I realized that the people you recruited didn't need to be bankers—they just need to be smart people who could assess the creditworthiness of the customer base.

The Referral Chain: From Josh to Rankin to Chris

We've found that the #1 best hiring source is to have direct, personal knowledge of an applicant long before a job interview. The #2 best source is a referral from a current employee whom you respect. Killer team members have a strong incentive to recruit more outstanding talent, and they know exactly what values you're looking for. At Lima One our employees became our best recruiters of new hires. Here's an example of how a chain reaction of referrals filled some essential early vacancies.

JW had met Josh Woodward a few years earlier while pitching fraternities to sign up with GadZeus. Josh had been a frat president at Clemson, and even as a college senior, he was impressively professional. JW made a point of staying in touch. Josh landed a corporate finance job at Bank of America in Charlotte, North Carolina, but by 2012 he felt stuck. His bank offered little opportunity for upward mobility, relying on an old-fashioned seniority system to promote people very slowly, no matter how qualified they were.

This was another example of a poor HR practice. Talented young people inevitably become hungry for recognition and rapid career advancement. It makes no sense to insist that everyone has to wait their turn, because high performers won't wait.

As with Cortney, our interviews and reference checks found that Josh had the values we wanted, including a chip on his shoulder because of the way his bank was treating him. As he recalls, "I wanted to work at a smaller, entrepreneurial company, and help build something great." He was intrigued by the opportunity to become our treasurer, even though he had no experience with real estate. On the other hand, he was wary of the risks of trading a secure job at a major bank for a startup that might not survive more than a year or two.

After some wooing, he couldn't resist the chance to help shape the destiny of a new company, and the opportunity for unlimited advancement. "At one point during the interview process," Josh recalls, "Top drove to Charlotte to have lunch with me. He looked me in the eye and said, with absolute conviction, 'We want you on the team.' I found those simple and direct actions and words to be quite powerful." Josh proved to be another killer on our team and later rose to become CFO. "Lima One presented that opportunity but, more specifically, I joined because of John and Top. It was clear from our first interactions that they were committed to achieving excellence by investing in people and building great teams."

Soon after Josh came on board, we told him that we urgently needed an operations expert. He said, "I know the perfect guy. One of my fraternity brothers, Rankin Blair, is a pure operations guy. And he's just as frustrated at his current job as I was."

We learned that Rankin's company was smaller than Josh's bank, but its HR practices were similar. Like Josh, Rankin felt stagnant, with no way to move up unless someone above him left. Rankin was an officer in the Army Reserves, and he felt so frustrated that he was seriously thinking of going back to active duty. "I was seeking a company that would offer an opportunity to advance my career," he recalls. "I knew joining an early-stage startup was a risk, but I knew that there would be exponentially more opportunity to develop than at a larger, more established company."

We interviewed him and found him to be just as impressive as Josh had said. Rankin had a passion for operations and the references to back it up. He jumped at the opportunity to become an underwriter, and eventually he rose to managing director of all operations for the company. He's also one of the biggest boosters of our hiring methods: "When I interview prospective candidates, they often ask, 'What are you most proud of about Lima One?' I am proud of the opportunity the company provides for its employees. Lima One Capital has taken a chance and invested in a lot in people that other companies would not have hired."

A few months after Rankin arrived, we needed to hire another underwriter to work on our growing influx of loan applications. Rankin told us that he knew the perfect guy, Chris Wilhoit.

We said, "Great, what's he doing now?"

"He's slinging carpets."

"What??"

Rankin explained: "Chris was an English major at Clemson, but he had a hard time finding a good job after graduation. His father is an anesthesiologist, so he could have just lived at home and sponged off his folks indefinitely. But he refused to do that—he wanted to be independent. So, he got a job installing carpets. His parents raised him to have a strong work ethic."

This was music to our ears. Hard worker, check. Grit to do an unpleasant job, check. Something to prove, check. Too proud to sponge off his parents, bonus points. "I had gone to work full-time at Cable Rugs doing stocking, assisting with some of the rug sales and rug deliveries," remembers Chris. "Basically, they needed young backs to lift those rugs and put them into people's cars. I was doing that full-time while also looking for a career." When we interviewed Chris, he more than lived up to Rankin's endorsement.

It occurred to us that other finance companies would have laughed at the idea of hiring an English major turned carpet installer to be a loan underwriter. They would have tossed his resume immediately. But we looked at it very differently. Loan underwriting isn't that hard if you put your mind to learning the process. Would we prefer some finance major who was happy to live off his parents and spend all his free time playing video games? Of course not—we'd rather hire a carpet slinger.

"What was important to me coming out of college was finding an organization where I could make an impact and help the organization grow," recalls Chris. "And I had a lot of respect for Josh and Rankin. The way they talked about the company and the founders' vision got me really excited about it. And I went all-in." Chris quickly picked up the basics of underwriting and started to thrive at his job. Before long he was originating hundreds of millions of dollars of high-quality loans. We later promoted him to launch and run our long-term finance division.

This chain reaction—Josh bringing in Rankin who brought in Chris—proved our theory that high performers are both willing and able to recruit more high performers. Like athletes on a team, everyone at a company is better off with the highest-quality teammates possible. The old saying "It takes one to know one" definitely applies. High performers never recommend low performers, even their closest friends, because they don't want to hurt the team or make themselves look bad.

As an extra incentive, we started paying our people for referrals. The reward started at $500 and grew over time to $3,000, as long as a new hire lasted at least 120 days. After all, if we'd be willing to pay some headhunter a 25 percent commission, why not redirect that budget to our own people? The tradition of recruiting by current employees endured through our last days at Lima One. Even in the final training class that Top taught for new hires, nine out of fifteen had been referred by a current employee.

If You Hire for Values, Diversity Will Take Care of Itself

The Marine Corps' model of recruitment leads to high levels of diversity—far more diversity than most civilian organizations now achieve through various Diversity, Equity, and Inclusion (DEI) initiatives. Marine recruiters make it clear that they want applicants of high character from all racial, ethnic, religious, and economic backgrounds, and that no one will be helped or hindered by their demographic origins.

Although the two of us look similar at first glance, our bond was born of shared values, not shared background. Top grew up as a white, Irish Catholic kid from Long Island, whose parents were blue-collar. JW grew up as a white Southern Baptist from South Carolina, whose family was upper-middle-class. Although our backgrounds were very different, our core values were the same. That's a microcosm of the Marine Corps, where Americans from every racial, ethnic, and religious group are represented.

We had it drilled into us that none of those differences mattered. Marines live together as equals, distinguished only by rank. We didn't pretend that the differences between us weren't real—that would have been naïve and unrealistic. But to become a powerful team we had to unite around our shared values and mission. Leaders who merely stress the differences between people fail to recognize the most important human traits. They can also do terrible harm to a team, a company, and even our country. This same lesson applies to diversity of thought.

Anyone who couldn't walk that talk—perhaps a white Marine who found it hard to take orders from a Latino sergeant—would quickly be gone. By the time we got to Iraq, we barely even noticed that our company commander was Mexican American, our executive officer was a good ol' boy from Missouri, and many of our company's NCOs and riflemen were black. None of it mattered.

At one point before we left Camp Lejeune for Ramadi, JW's platoon included both a black working-class squad leader from Atlanta and a young white Marine from one of the wealthiest families in Alabama. The latter's father once sent a private jet to pick him up for a weekend of liberty. He had joined the Marines to prove that he wasn't just a spoiled rich kid, and he took orders from his squad leader just like everyone else. It didn't matter how much money their respective families had in the outside world, or what the history of their ancestors had been.

We took that attitude to Lima One. We made it very clear that all decisions about hiring, training, supervision, and promotion had to be made on objective evaluations of merit, without any kind of discrimination. People who were not comfortable with diversity weren't welcome. True, equitable diversity is the product of holding everyone accountable to the same values and standards. "I was black, and you guys were white," notes Cortney Newmans. "But anyone that came in the door, we were all treated the same, no matter what. It was because of our core values and our belief in hard work."

A couple of years after Cortney joined us, his grandmother passed away. We both went to Macon for the funeral, as we often do to show support for our employees. We might have been the only two white people at that funeral, but that didn't matter one bit. Cortney's extended family and friends made us feel completely welcome, because they could tell that we shared the same values. We shared a good meal together with great stories after the funeral; strangers became friends because of our shared admiration for Cortney.

Marines don't ignore race—in fact we're even able to joke about it. Before we deployed to Ramadi, Lima Company pulled a hilarious prank on Lieutenant Sherman, who was the last platoon commander to check into the company because he maxed out his vacation days before joining his new unit. Staff Sergeant Anglade, who was Lieutenant Sherman's new platoon sergeant, asked Captain Barela to switch uniforms on the day Lieutenant Sherman finally joined us. Staff Sergeant Anglade, who was black, pretended to be the company commander, and vice versa.

"Captain," Anglade yelled at Lieutenant Sherman for taking all those vacation days, and then called him a racist when Lieutenant Sherman tried to defend himself. "I was sitting in the office," recalls Staff Sergeant Anglade. "I was messing with him. I said, 'What's going on? You don't like black people?'" He was really starting to sweat when we admitted the prank. In a truly merit-driven, equal-opportunity organization, being able to kid around about race is healthier than pretending it doesn't exist.

These same principles should apply not only to racial diversity, but also to diversity of thought. Today, our country has become so polarized that tolerance of diverging viewpoints and ideologies has mostly become a thing of the past. Instead of engaging in civil discussions about issues, large sectors of our society have digressed into name-calling, public shaming, or "canceling" alternate views. We urge you not to let this trend infect your organization. Just as we are all Americans at our core, regardless of our political beliefs, your team of killers needs to accept that the organization's mission matters more than partisanship. It's appropriate to ask everyone to check their politics at the door during business hours.

If you hire exclusively for core values and core competence, and push aside any bias based on credentials, industry experience, demographics, or politics, you will have a huge advantage over nearly every organization you compete with.

CHAPTER 5

TRAIN FOR CULTURE FIRST

An Enlisted Man's Journey (Top)

As a new recruit in 1989, I spent thirteen weeks at Parris Island, South Carolina, the location for basic training for every Marine east of the Mississippi. I immediately noticed the diversity of my group. I was a Long Island kid thrown together with about forty-five other recruits from Ohio, Louisiana, Florida, North Carolina, and so on. Sometimes I had trouble understanding their accents, but in a very short time the process turned us into a cohesive unit. The drill instructors made it clear that if we didn't work together, none of us would survive basic training.

The physical part of training actually wasn't as tough as I had expected from movies and TV, because I'd been an athlete in high school. I could handle the running and push-ups. The hardest part, believe it or not, was not laughing at the drill instructors when they made fun of us. They hit us with the most obscene insults, way beyond anything I'd ever heard, which always broke my composure. I kept getting in trouble because I couldn't focus during those insults as we stood at attention.

I later realized that their attempts to distract us were a key part of our training. What we would eventually see and hear in combat would be a lot more distracting than anything they could possibly yell at us, and we needed to build up our discipline.

The other key part of basic was how the drill instructors stressed the core values of honor, courage, and commitment. They made it clear that we weren't going to learn about combat until we demonstrated the character of true Marines. The burden was on us to prove that we deserved to wear the uniform, which represented a long legacy of glory and honor. Did we have what it takes to uphold that legacy, even if we had to give our lives in the process? A surprising amount of time was spent on teaching us Marine Corps history—the heroes who came before us and those who made the ultimate sacrifice in battle. We were required to memorize the most famous Marines who were awarded the Congressional Medal of Honor, names like Dan Daly, John Basilone, Jimmie Howard, Wesley Fox, and many others. This tradition continues today.

They also set up a sense of competition with the other services—stoking the idea that everyone in the other branches was jealous of us. They said the Marines were always the first branch sent into any hot spot in the world, the first to come under enemy fire. America's enemies hated us openly, and our colleagues in the other branches resented us. But that was fine—it was us against the world.

There wasn't much time to celebrate after surviving boot camp, because we were immediately sent to combat training at Camp Geiger, North Carolina. This four-week program taught us the fundamentals of being Marine riflemen, which we had been told was the core skill for any Marine. No matter what rank you were, you had to be able to set up and hold a rifle position and hit your targets with accuracy and consistency. This new phase would be just as make-or-break as boot camp.

Combat training was much tougher than basic training, both physically and mentally. Some guys who did very well at boot camp were suddenly in trouble. The entire four weeks are spent out in the field, which makes it physically demanding. The purpose of combat training is to teach the Marine Corps war-fighting ethos, basic tenets of maneuver warfare, and the mental, moral, and physical resiliency needed in combat to accomplish the mission.

Because I had volunteered to go into the infantry, the third phase of my training was another nine weeks at Infantry School, also at Camp Geiger. At this point, the lessons were getting much more technical. Most of our time was out in the field, with combat instructors demonstrating one-on-one how to handle our weapons and conduct combat patrols. By building on top of the skills and knowledge we had already mastered in basic training and combat training, Infantry School dramatically elevated our competence. (These days infantry Marines skip combat training and go directly to a longer version of Infantry School, but the sequence of instruction is roughly the same.)

By the time I left the country in 1990 for my first combat deployment to Kuwait, I felt very well prepared.

The Three Kinds of Training

Once you've assembled a team of killers, the next key step is training them. This can be a lot harder than many leaders assume, if they fail to grasp what Top discovered during boot camp: there are really three very different kinds of training. The Marine Corps trains for culture first, followed by fundamental skills, followed by the specialized skills. To define those terms:

CULTURE = the values, history, priorities, and standards of the organization. This kind of training should take priority as the bedrock foundation, because if a new hire can't or won't accept the expectations of the culture, it doesn't matter how proficient they are at any skills.

FUNDAMENTAL SKILLS AND KNOWLEDGE = the basics of how the organization operates and the core competencies that drive its success. Some new hires will be better than others at these skills, but a baseline of competence is nonnegotiable. An example of this kind of training is the idea that "Every Marine is a rifleman."

SPECIALIZED SKILLS AND KNOWLEDGE = The specific expertise required to perform a specific role within the organization. This might include anything from making a cappuccino to punting a football to filing a legal brief.

But this sequence is the opposite of the way most companies onboard their new hires. Corporate America tends to put specialized skills first, either by making them a requirement for getting hired or by immediately training new recruits to perform the specific tasks required for their jobs. Teaching the fundamentals of the business is usually done informally, in bits and pieces over time. Teaching the culture, values, and history of the organization might not happen at all, or it might get boiled down to a one-page handout, because it's the lowest priority. In many companies, new employees absorb the culture by osmosis, and the company's stated values can easily get lost in the shuffle.

The Corps feels so strongly about this training sequence that you have to clear the bar of the first two kinds of training before you can even call yourself a Marine. That's another example of a Marine tradition that doesn't match the other branches. If you join the Army, they start to call you "Soldier" on day one of basic training, so you'll begin to think of yourself as a soldier. Likewise, Navy recruits are immediately called "Sailor" and Air Force recruits are immediately called "Airman."

But in the Marines, you are called "Recruit" all through boot camp, or "Candidate" all through Officer Candidate School. The title of "Marine" is an honor you must earn by proving your grasp of the Corps' culture and basic skills. Then and only then are you rewarded with your Eagle, Globe & Anchor (EGA) pin—the first official recognition for any new Marine. JW recalls the importance of that pin:

When I went through OCS, some of the candidates in my class were enlisted Marines now trying to become officers. They already had their EGA and were treated differently because of it. For instance, there's a tradition that Marines say "happy birthday" to each other on November 10, to celebrate the founding of the Corps on November 10, 1775. That day at OCS, the NCOs training us singled out the enlisted to say, "Happy birthday, Marine." But the rest of us weren't allowed to say it, and no one was allowed to say it to us. I felt jealous and even more eager to earn my EGA.

An Officer Candidate's Journey (JW)

Officer Candidates School at Quantico, Virginia, was a ten-week course that focused on endurance, Marine Corps values, leadership principles, and the standards expected of an officer. Weapons, combat skills, and military tactics were given relatively little attention. In fact, we didn't fire a single live round of ammunition during those ten weeks, just blanks. The Marines set up OCS to challenge our resolve, character, and leadership potential. If we couldn't clear those hurdles and show that we embraced Marine culture, we would quickly be gone. It didn't matter (yet) how well we could shoot an M4 or set up an 81mm mortar.

We had little interaction with the officer in charge of our platoon of candidates, because nearly everything was run by staff NCOs. Those staff sergeants and gunnery sergeants were the most professional and effective teachers I've ever seen. They taught us exactly what it means to be a Marine, making sure we grasped the values demanded of us and the standards to which we would be held. In the process, these amazing teachers inspired us to respect and admire the senior enlisted ranks, which stayed with all of us when we went on to command platoons.

In addition to stressing culture and values, OCS prioritized mental toughness. We had to do a lot of physical training under sleep deprivation, to see if we could handle serious stress for days (later weeks) at a time. Many in my class couldn't cut it; more than a third either quit or were kicked out. We could see that the Marines treated OCS as a filtering process as well as a training process. Even though the program had extremely high admissions standards, there was no way for recruiters to be 100 percent sure who would have the character and competence to serve as Marine officers. They made OCS tough enough to weed out anyone who lacked intense commitment and grit.

Those of us who graduated got our EGA and second lieutenant's bars, but we were not even close to finished with our training. The second phase took place at the Basic School (TBS), also at Quantico. This was six months of increasingly complex training for new officers, with the goal of making us qualified to lead an infantry platoon. TBS challenged us to absorb tons of new information and the fundamental skills of a Marine officer.

Finally, the third phase of our training—for specialized skills— was the Infantry Officer Course (IOC), another thirteen weeks of the hardest training I've ever experienced. It was about 90 percent fieldwork, applying everything we had learned to simulated combat scenarios. It's no exaggeration that I'd rather go back to real combat in Ramadi than go back to combat training at IOC. The captains who served as our instructors exposed us to the worst situations they could imagine. They were outstanding at mentoring us and demonstrating everything one-on-one. They also earned our respect by sharing every hardship that they expected us to endure in the field.

Civilians often assume that the hardest part of military training is the physical testing. But if you're in very good shape, a ten-mile run isn't much of a hardship. The truly stressful part was managing our thoughts and emotions in the face of the unknown. IOC taught us that in combat you can never really know what's coming at you or what will be expected from you. If you can't handle that kind of mental and emotional stress, it won't matter how many miles you can run.

For instance, at one point we were out in the field for extended war games, under grueling conditions of heat, rain, sleep deprivation, and minimal rations. We were not told how long the exercise would last. After six days a group of trucks showed up and we loaded into them, assuming that the war games were over and we were returning to base. We felt tremendous elation and relief—for about sixty seconds. Then the trucks pulled to a stop again. The captains began yelling, "Just kidding! Get out of the trucks! You still have days to go in the field!" Our elation quickly turned to depression, and we remained exhausted and miserable for another four days.

Adapting Marine Training for Business

When we designed our training programs for Lima One Capital, we emulated the Marine Corps for all three phases. First and foremost, we created a business version of boot camp to teach new hires our mission, values, and standards, and help them bond with their new colleagues. Second, we taught the basic skills of our business, the equivalent to "Every Marine is a rifleman." Then and only then, we trained new hires in the specialized skills they needed to do their jobs. This last phase concluded with a powerful Marine training tactic called left seat/right seat turnover.

We often hear skepticism from other leaders about our training methods. The pushback usually sounds something like this: "Our company is not the Marine Corps. This much training is unnecessary. It will cost too much money and take too much time." These critics are right that our training probably costs more and takes more time than theirs. But they're dead wrong that it isn't worth it. Great training elevates the two most important employee metrics: performance and retention. The Marine way of training will drive better results from your team members and will inspire them to stay with your company much longer.

We confirmed this when we sent former Lima One employees a questionnaire about their experiences. In response to being asked, "What are you most proud of about your time at Lima One?" we expected most to talk about the company's incredible growth or financial milestones. Instead, nearly everyone stressed the company's values and culture. A few typical responses:

DREW FITZPATRICK: "The values upon which the company was founded, the culture which was maintained throughout my tenure, and the transparency/directness provided by leadership."

BARRETT CLAYTON: "The company has quadrupled in size since I have been a part of the team and the strong values have remained. I have never been, nor would I expect to be put in a situation that would compromise those values."

BILL MCDONALD: "The high standard of integrity. This is truly a Marine trait and Lima One embraced it, as did I. It was a culture of honor, integrity, and execution."

JOSH WOODWARD: "I am most proud of the culture that we built. The patterns of behaviors that we encouraged and others we did not tolerate."

JACK MCGINNESS: "Lima One's greatest asset and competitive edge was the aggregate character and virtues of its people. Its core value to me was the idea that one could compete in a marketplace with a dishonest and sleazy reputation by bringing a radical sense of honesty, transparency, and character into that marketplace."

We share these quotes not to boast, but to show that training for culture first can pay off far beyond your expectations.

Phase One: Values and Culture

The first step in our new employee orientation consisted of two briefings: the Lima One investor presentation and our Ramadi deployment presentation. We believed that both were so vital that without exception at least one of us (usually both) delivered them. They took about three hours, including breaks and time for questions. "Intimidating and

Billion Dollar Party on October 9, 2018, for Lima One Capital employees, cele-
brating reaching $1 billion in loan originations.

refreshing at the same time" is how Brandy Cogsdill described her first
day of training. "It was a different approach than what I had experienced
anywhere else. It wasn't just about the business tasks—you learned who
they were and what Lima One really stood for."

The investor presentation—the same deck of slides that we used to
persuade investors to trust us with hundreds of millions of dollars—
detailed every aspect of our business. It gave a comprehensive overview
of our history, organization, loan products, underwriting process, sales
channels, and financials. We continually updated the slides as the
company grew, so the numbers were always up-to-date. *Here's how we
raise money and how we allocate it to our borrowers. Here's the current
state of our loan portfolio, overhead expenses, growth projections. Here are
the major competitors we're facing.*

By the end of the investor briefing, our new hires understood more
about their company than most people elsewhere do after several years.
"During the investor brief, I could tell Top was passionate about what
the company was doing and the importance of making good loans for

our investors," recalls Barrett Clayton. "I left that section with an understanding that every single loan mattered, and to treat our investors' money as if it was my own."

Our candor often surprised our new employees. We knew it was extremely unusual to present this level of financial detail to entry-level people, especially on their first day. But we did it because sharing confidential information generates a sense of shared mission.* Putting all those confidential financial details on the screen showed our new hires that we trusted them. In return, we expected them to prove themselves worthy of our trust.

Next, we gave our Ramadi deployment presentation, which summarized our service in the Marines, our deployment in Ramadi, and the April 17, 2006, attack on OPVA. We included the al-Qaeda propaganda video in which they filmed the suicide bomber driving the dump truck and detonating it at our base. We explained that Lima Company taught us so much about what makes an organization effective, while also giving us perspective on our current challenges, as a scrappy underdog in the world of real estate finance. We really wanted our new employees to share that perspective. No matter how tough things might get at work, at least none of us had to worry about getting blown up by an IED or RPG. Even the hardest sales call couldn't compare to trying to convince Iraqi civilians to risk their lives and family's lives by helping the Marines defeat al-Qaeda.

During the Ramadi briefing, we presented the values that we considered the foundation of Lima One. Of course we expected hard work and resilience, but so do lots of other companies. What set us apart, we explained, was that we were dead serious about expecting complete honesty and integrity. The Marines taught us that character is doing the right thing when no one else is looking. Mistakes made in good faith would often be forgivable, but lying or cheating, especially to cover up a mistake, would be a firing offense. We explained that lies of omission

---

* We'll further explore this tactic in Chapter 7.

(failing to report something) are just as bad as lies of commission. If we can't trust you, we can't work with you. Period.

"The Ramadi briefing sticks with me to this day," says Josh Woodward. "I remember watching the video of the jihadist driving an explosive-laden truck towards OPVA. The passion and intensity with which John and Top shared the details of their experiences in Iraq and their commitment to their comrades set a distinct tone. I immediately understood their discipline and execution, and what they expected of us as employees."

Our values led naturally to the guiding principles of our culture, the rules that we expected everyone to live by every day. These were an early version of the key strategies you're reading about in this book, such as: do everything for a reason; empower your fireteams; be blunt and direct; think long-term; and avoid comfort-based decisions.

"After the briefings, my desire to contribute to the company increased tenfold," recalls Drew Fitzpatrick. "What initially began as an opportunity to build a career in a different field quickly became a mission to make a meaningful impact on what John and Top had built."

Those orientation briefings got good feedback, but not every new hire loved them. A few must have thought Lima One was too much like a cult, because our onboarding process was so unconventional and so focused on values and culture. But in ten years only a handful of people ever quit because of the Ramadi briefing. One day we were presenting to a group of twelve, but following a break only eleven were back in the room. One of the trainees simply said, "David quit." We later found out that during the break, David had walked up to our director of HR, Katie. She cheerfully asked him, "Can I help you with anything? Need directions to the break room?"

His reply: "No, thanks. I just wanted to let you know that I'm leaving. I realize that this isn't the place for me." He walked out and we never heard from him again. On the very rare occasions when something like that happened, we were fine with it. We'd much rather have someone quit on day one because they don't align with the culture than have them quit on day 90, 120, or 365, after we've invested in training them. The goal of our training wasn't to weed out bad fits who accidentally made it through our recruitment process. But as with Marine boot camp, it was a valuable bonus that training acted as a backup filter.

Phase Two: Fundamental Skills Training

We thought hard about defining the Lima One equivalent of "Every Marine is a rifleman" during phase two of training. What was the fundamental knowledge of our business that everyone needed to understand, no matter what role they were about to play at the company?

We landed on "Every Lima One employee is an underwriter." Underwriting loans was the essence of our business, so we explained to new hires that if they didn't understand that process, they wouldn't really understand our company. And that deficit of knowledge would hurt their results in any other department, such as sales or customer service.

After each new employee heard those first two briefings, they attended a week of sessions that led them step by step through the underwriting process. We started by dissecting our loan application and how we decided whether to approve a loan, based on a combination of financial, real estate, and personal criteria. A qualified buyer who wanted a bad property had to be rejected, just like an unqualified buyer seeking a great property. Then we explained the processes for closing a loan, servicing it, and dealing with a client at risk of default. We tried to keep things interesting with stories of unusual clients. New hires felt a real sense of accomplishment when they passed their final written test at the conclusion of this Underwriting 101 crash course.

Some of our accountants or customer service reps would be puzzled when they learned about our training plan. Why should they have to know how to underwrite a loan? We explained that if you don't understand loans, at least on a basic level, you can't fully understand your role in accounting or customer service or any other department. Justin Thompson describes the impact this training process had on his future performance:

I was the marketing guy, so going in I expected to just learn the basics of the company and industry and then be let loose to do my job. I was wrong. I fully underwrote numerous loans and was expected to be able to manually calculate rate and leverage. I was exposed to every aspect of the company, with enough hands-on training to be a loan underwriter or business development rep. I would have been mediocre at best in either role, but it underscores the time and resources put into making me a well-rounded employee. That exposure was extremely important throughout my years at Lima One.

Fundamental skills training especially paid off in 2015, when we launched a new "Rental 30" program for longer-term property loans (up to thirty years), in contrast to the shorter loans we had been originating up to that point. The program was much more popular than we anticipated, leaving us unprepared for a flood of new loan applications, plus high demand from Wall Street to securitize our loans. We didn't want any delays in the origination process to tarnish our exceptional reputation for closing all qualifying loans within ten days after an application.

The only way to get through this crunch without dropping our standard of service was by relying on the cross-training of our entire staff. We were able to turn our marketing team, business development team, and some of our sales team into temporary loan underwriters. Even our head of marketing, head of sales, and CFO were screening loan applications part-time, while our administrative assistants took customer service calls. Everyone felt great about being part of the solution as we cleared the surge in applications.

Lima One was hardly the only company teaching everyone the same core skills, even if unrelated to their main job. When JW got to know the CEO of Waffle House, Walt Ehmer, he learned that the restaurant chain uses a similar approach for its forty thousand employees. At Waffle House, the motto could easily be "Everyone is a server." Ehmer, a very humble, very effective leader, says, "Servers build our business. They are the face of our business and everybody else is a supporting cast. Our number one job is to make our servers successful. When they're successful, we're successful."

Ehmer requires every Waffle House employee to put in several shifts in one of its 2,000+ restaurants. Everyone has to put on an apron just like any entry-level worker—taking orders from customers, cooking, cleaning up, taking out the trash. Even if you were hired as a vice president of operations or a marketing director, you first must see the world through the eyes of a frontline worker. "Everybody starts learning how to wait tables and learning how to cook," Ehmer says. "The model is, you do every job here from cooking to waiting tables, cleaning and inventory. And when you get your next job, you are therefore a much better teacher to the people you now are responsible for." Ehmer believes that this policy was vital to keeping the culture of Waffle House consistent as the chain continued to grow.

Even a few traditional corporations are seeing the value in starting people with fundamental training about their business. JW recalls:

> When I did that management training program at Michelin, prior to joining the Marine Corps, one thing that impressed me was that they expect everyone to understand tires. It didn't matter if you were hired as an accountant or an IT person—you had to learn how tires were made, what distinguished different types, how to repair them and change them. Everyone had to be at least somewhat of an expert in their core product.

Phase Three: Specialized Training via Left Seat/Right Seat Turnover

The Marines use left seat/right seat turnover during deployments to enable one unit to pass along very specific details about a battle space to the next unit that's about to replace them. The phrase originates from a driver of a Jeep who explained the terrain and another Marine in the shotgun seat, who absorbed all the details. We experienced left seat/right seat twice in Ramadi, during the first two weeks and last two weeks of our deployment.

When we arrived in March 2006, our company (Lima 3/8) was taking over from Lima Company, Third Battalion, Seventh Marines (aka Lima 3/7). For the next two weeks we shared Snakepit with them, with everyone in Lima 3/8 meeting daily with our counterparts in Lima 3/7. Our platoons shared patrols as they showed us the nuances of our sector, especially the most dangerous spots. They explained the tactics of the insurgents, and what Lima 3/7 had been doing to counter them. They also introduced us to key allies, such as the local Iraqi police and the Iraqi Security Force (ISF). Those introductions were crucial because part of our mission was to train the ISF to assume more responsibility for maintaining peace in our sector.

During left seat/right seat, at first the veteran unit does the actual work and makes all the decisions, while the new unit watches and learns. Then, little by little, the new unit does more work, while receiving constructive feedback from the veterans. By the end of the two-week transition, the new unit should be doing everything and should have enough mastery that the veterans hardly need to correct anything.

JW will never forget his first left seat/right seat ride around our sector:

> The day after we arrived in Ramadi, one of the platoon commanders from Lima 3/7 took me on patrol with a section of Humvees. For me personally, this was the finish line of four years of trying to get into combat. But when I left the security of Snakepit and crossed into the unprotected streets of Ramadi for the first time, I didn't feel any sense of achievement. Instead, all I could think was, "What the hell am I doing here?" After we stopped and exited our vehicles, I heard snapping noises overhead and asked the other

lieutenant what that sound was. "You're getting shot at," he replied. Fortunately, my training kicked in and I calmly went to work.

Seven months later, our departure from Ramadi mirrored our arrival, except now we were the experts showing a new company the lay of the land. We took a new set of officers and NCOs out on patrols and explained how we had built up good relations with the locals, and what they needed to do to keep building on our progress. We explained all the tactics we had developed for fighting effectively in Ramadi and developing actionable intelligence on insurgents. After two weeks, that new company was ready to take over.

Years later, we copied this process almost exactly at Lima One Capital. After each new hire learned our culture and values and then learned how to be an underwriter, he or she was matched with an experienced employee in their department. The new hire would watch the veteran for a few days, observing all the nuances of the job, asking as many questions as necessary. Then the new person started doing parts of the job, with the experienced employee observing and giving feedback. The transition would continue until the veteran felt that the newcomer was ready to fly solo, whether that required just a couple of days or up to two weeks.

Another, less obvious benefit of left seat/right seat is the effect it has on the trainers. It empowers them with leadership and trust, and it gives them a feeling of ownership in the success of the new hire. That has tremendous impact on developing new leaders in the organization.

We still smile about one Friday afternoon when the two of us were discussing an important business decision, or possibly just the latest woes of Top's beloved New York Giants. We heard a knock on JW's office door from Kim, an underwriter who had been with Lima One for about ten months. She said, "Sorry to interrupt but I just wanted to thank you guys."

"For what?" we responded.

"For giving me the opportunity to train one of the new hires. It means a lot that you would have that kind of faith in me, since I've only been here less than a year." That comment made our week. Years later, Kim is still thriving at Lima One.

Good Training Leaves Room for Innovation

Here's one final conclusion from our many experiences with training, both military and business. Some leaders avoid systematic training because they worry that too much training squashes creativity. They fear that if they give their people too much detail about how to do their jobs, they'll stick to the status quo instead of exploring new ways to improve the business.

We've found that the opposite is true. People who get too little training, or the wrong kind of training, tend to flounder unproductively. They need much longer to figure out the basics of their job—including the core values, standards, and expectations of the organization. All of that unproductive time and effort makes them far less likely to test potential new strategies or tactics. Well-trained employees, in contrast, feel secure that they understand exactly what the organization values and expects of them. This clarity and security free them up to apply their creativity to new and better approaches, without violating the leadership team's standards.

Fixing the way we train employees is vital to repairing corporate America's misguided practices. With better training, you can create a strong culture, give everyone a strong foundation in fundamental skills, and develop experts who will shine in their specialized areas.

All of these benefits dovetail neatly with the benefits of empowering junior employees, which we'll explore in our next chapter.

CHAPTER 6

EMPOWER YOUR
FIRETEAMS

The Universal Challenge of Teams

Dysfunctional teams seem to be a universal problem. We bet you could tell us many stories of serving in organizations where fundamental conflicts within teams never seem to get resolved. Where meetings drag on and on. Where the personal agendas of individual team members undermine the overall mission. Where the leader seems powerless to get everyone rowing in the same direction.

A big part of this dynamic, we've found, is the size of a group that's being asked to act as a cohesive team. Large committees, by their nature, disempower individuals and increase the risks of passivity and distraction. When you're just one of fifteen people on a team, it's easy to assume that someone else is solving problems and taking responsibility for results. Maybe you start to zone out during meetings. Maybe you complain privately to your friend about dumb decisions, but never speak up to the leader or the full group. Maybe everyone freezes during a crisis. Maybe you get so discouraged that you have to quit.

The Marines must have figured out these truths of interpersonal psychology many decades ago, because they approach teams in a very different way than the corporate world. This chapter will show you how they use teams as a tool to driving outstanding results, develop new leaders, and foster strong cohesion at all times, even during—especially during—moments of crisis. It all starts with the four-man fireteam, the smallest organization unit in the Marine Corps.

Before we get into explaining why fireteam dynamics solve the universal challenge of teams, let us show you an extreme example of those dynamics during a life-or-death crisis.

Fireteams under Fire

On the hot, muggy night of August 2, 2006, just after 2200 (10:00 p.m.), Lima Company's Fourth Platoon left OPVA to conduct a mission deep into central Ramadi. As usual, the platoon was split up into three squads, and each squad was split into three fireteams, composed of four Marines each. Accompanying Fourth Platoon were two squads from Second Platoon, one squad from First Platoon, Captain Barela, and Lima Company's adopted dog, Molly.

In the lead position that night was Fourth Platoon's Second Squad, led by Corporal Joe Tomci. At just twenty-one, Corporal Tomci was an outstanding Marine from Stow, Ohio. He was universally loved and respected as one of the company's greatest natural leaders. "Tomci was a very strong leader," recalls his radioman, Lance Corporal Ryan Walblay. "He was somebody you looked up to. He was always keeping us in high spirits, no matter how shitty the mission was, no matter how tired we were. He would motivate us to keep going." Corporal Tomci was the kind of guy who wrote a weekly letter to his local elementary school back home. Lance Corporal Garner from First Platoon, who was on that night's mission, says simply, "I consider Tomci one of the best Marines I ever met. I thought he was the best in the company."

August 6 was the first time that any Marines from our battalion

Corporal Joe Tomci with local Iraqis while conducting a census of the population in Ramadi, Iraq, 2006.

were patrolling this neighborhood. After five months of implementing our counterinsurgency strategy, much of Lima Company's original area of operations had become peaceful, with insurgents migrating to the east. To build on this success, Captain Barela asked to have our area of operations expanded to the northeast and southeast. Our battalion commander agreed to his request, and we handed over a substantial portion of our original territory to the control of the Iraqi Army, while Lima Company focused on more dangerous turf. We even gave up our main base, Snakepit, to live full-time at OPVA.

As Second Squad moved out from OPVA, dispersed Marines bounded across intersections, trying to dodge the few streetlights that still worked while keeping their eyes open for any piece of trash or rubble that might camouflage an IED. With the typical Marine carrying fifty to seventy-five pounds of gear, and temperatures at night in the nineties, foot patrols required an extreme combination of physical endurance and intense mental focus. It took about forty minutes for Fourth Platoon and

Captain Barela to reach their objective, about a mile and a half to the northeast. Once there, the three squads from First and Second Platoons set up in overwatch, meaning that they took over buildings or homes to help protect the Marines in Fourth Platoon, who were in and out of houses while Captain Barela talked with local Iraqi leaders.

After about two and a half hours, it was time to return to base. The squad leaders from Fourth Platoon huddled and determined that Corporal Tomci's squad would once again take the lead going back to OPVA. The Marines quickly traversed roads and alleys and were about ten minutes from base when Corporal Tomci radioed, "I'm pushing back towards Little Elbow and Ice." Those were street names of an intersection just north of OPVA. Corporal Tomci's lead fireteam headed west towards Ice Street, to make the final turn south to OPVA, with Corporal Tomci and Lance Corporal Walblay right behind them. Just then, a massive IED exploded, sending smoke, dust, and deadly shrapnel flying. Lance Corporal Walblay recalls that terrifying experience:

> When the explosion happens and you're that close to a massive IED, the sound hits you first as a concussion, like a thunder and lightning strike in your ear. I got lifted off my feet and thrown a couple yards down the street. Then you get ringing in your ears. Then you feel whatever pain comes from your injury. But then it becomes so painful that you just don't feel it anymore. At that point the adrenaline is kicking in and you just have to suck it up and try to make it through.

Lance Corporal Walblay's left leg went completely numb, and he realized his left foot was hit badly. He rolled onto his stomach and pointed his rifle down the street, expecting enemy fighters. With a thick cloud of black smoke covering the street, he was unable to see any of his fellow Marines and thought he might be the only one hit. Unfortunately, the IED had exploded directly under Corporal Tomci, instantly severing his leg, causing massive bleeding, and rendering him unconscious. Second

Squad's leader was out of the fight. Making matters worse, the platoon commander for Fourth Platoon was paralyzed by fear and unable to carry out his responsibilities.

Back at OPVA, Lieutenant Sherman and Sergeant MacGregor were in the combat operations center (COC) when they heard the blast. As they tried to radio the distressed platoon commander, they received no response. "He couldn't formulate," recalls Lieutenant Sherman. "We're like, 'Where are you? What's happened? What's going on?' All I needed was a location, but I couldn't get it out of him."

A routine patrol was now a chaotic combat zone, and the three fireteams that reported to Corporal Tomci now had no one to issue orders to them. Corporal Tomci's platoon commander was suddenly nowhere near the action. How would Second Squad survive this crisis?

The Rule of Threes and Fours

The four-man rifle fireteam evolved over decades to deliver both superior effectiveness in combat plus invaluable opportunities for NCOs to hone their leadership skills.

In the Marines, a corporal or lance corporal leading a fireteam has full responsibility for three other lives: a rifleman, an automatic rifleman or machine gunner, and an assistant automatic rifleman. The leader decides the team's movements, identifies targets, and issues commands when it's time to fire. In combat, he carries an M16 with a grenade launcher attached, so he can also serve as the fireteam's grenadier.*

All of these roles require quick thinking and the self-confidence to give orders in life-or-death situations, such as that August 6 ambush. Being a fireteam leader is a huge responsibility for a young Marine who might have only eighteen to twenty-four months of experience at that

---

* Different units will have variations in weapons, but the leadership principles are the same.

point. He's in charge of making sure the team operates as a cohesive unit, carries out its mission, and returns to base safely.

Three fireteams make up a squad, each reporting to a squad leader who is usually a sergeant. At the next level, three squads ladder up to a platoon, led by a lieutenant and a platoon sergeant. Three or four platoons ladder up to a company, led by a captain. Three rifle companies make up a battalion, and three battalions make up a regiment. There are some variations to this structure in certain situations. But the core principle, which we call the rule of threes and fours, is simple: leaders should never be responsible for more than four subordinates, or they will begin to lose effectiveness. This holds true all the way up to the top of the chain of command.

The rule of threes and fours is the solution to the universal challenge of teams that we described above. Small teams tend to get demonstrably better results than big teams. They enjoy clearer focus, stronger cohesion, and much less internal conflict. They're more likely to act quickly and decisively during a crisis. As a result, the more experience you get serving on a small team, and then leading a small team, the better you'll become at making consequential decisions and taking ownership of problems.

Now that you understand this background, let's go back to that tragic night in Ramadi.*

Fireteams Jump into the Void

Upon hearing the loud explosion, Corporal Daniel Tarantino, squad leader for Third Squad, immediately feared the worst. As he recalls, "When Tomci's radio transmission got cut, my heart sank. We sprinted towards that intersection faster than any of us had ever run in our lives." Corporal Tarantino arrived to find Corporal Tomci and Lance Corporal Walblay at what the Marines call a casualty collection point. Lance

---

* Neither of us was a direct eyewitness to the ambush. But we were close enough to Fourth Platoon to hear the explosion and the radio communications. We got the full story from multiple Marines on the patrol and on the scene.

Corporal Carson Randall had picked up both Corporal Tomci and Lance Corporal Walblay from the middle of the street and got them to a better location where the corpsman could treat them.

Meanwhile, Corporal Tomci's three fireteam leaders, including Private First Class David Seymour, were already responding by setting up firing positions against any potential follow-on attacks. Any insurgents who tried to fire on them would have been immediately taken out.

Corporal Tarantino stepped in to assume command of the situation, telling Seymour to take *his* squad (which, tragically, was no longer Corporal Tomci's squad) and secure the far side of the intersection. Corporal Tarantino then fired his red-star cluster, a signal flare that indicates a mass casualty requiring immediate QRF (quick reaction force) support and casualty evacuation.

As Marines from First Platoon arrived to assist with providing security and treating the casualties, Captain Barela also reached the site of the explosion. He found Corporal Tomci unconscious as the corpsmen worked to stop his bleeding. Lieutenant Sherman and Sergeant MacGregor then arrived with Third Platoon, having raced from OPVA to provide the QRF and the casualty evacuation. While driving the wounded to a hospital called Charlie Med, about two miles away, corpsmen worked hard to keep all three of Corporal Tomci's tourniquets secure. Despite the heroic efforts of everyone on the scene, Corporal Tomci died at the hospital. As word spread, the entire company felt deep loss and devastation. One Marine recalled that hearing the news "was like getting hit with a hammer."

As terrible as it was that the platoon commander froze, it was just as impressive that the squad and fireteam leaders instantly stepped up to fill the gap. Their courage and quick thinking prevented the crisis from escalating into a catastrophe, if the insurgents had been free to attack after the chaos caused by the IED. As Lieutenant Jason Clark, the company's executive officer, summed it up, "It ended up being [the platoon commander's] subordinates who had to push things through.

That's why we say, 'You have to be able to do the job of two leaders above you.' I think that night we proved it. We had very junior fireteam leaders stepping up and making squad-level and platoon-level decisions, because their superior was mentally out of the fight at that point."

The fireteam training process had prepared these junior leaders to stay cool as they figured out what needed to be done, move their men into a proper security position, treat the casualties, and complete the mission to the best of their ability.

Big Teams Create Overstressed Leaders and Frustrated Workers

In contrast to the rule of threes and fours in a Marine unit, consider the typical business unit in a big company. The number of direct reports for a single executive often approaches seven to ten. Even twelve to fifteen direct reports are fairly common, especially for department heads who use head count as a marker of status within the company. It's an easy and public way to signal, "Mine is bigger than yours."

But as direct head count grows, even the best executives are increasingly prone to distraction, conflicting priorities, and burnout. Their email inboxes become a nonstop flood of questions, updates, and requests for approval. They find that the bottom of the inbox can never be reached, no matter how many nights and weekends they put in. Their calendars become overstuffed with nonstop meetings to give their subordinates attention and guidance, if not to micromanage them completely.

Given all this pressure on their time, these executives find themselves paying less and less attention to long-term challenges and opportunities, as they fall into permanent triage mode. They're just trying to put out enough fires and solve enough problems to get through the day, week, quarter, or year. Forget about strategic thinking or proactively coming up with new ideas—they never have time for that stuff. If you ask this kind of executive how work is going, they always reply, "BUSY!" But being

Corporal Joe Tomci with local Iraqis while conducting a census of the population in Ramadi, Iraq, 2006.

busy without focusing on true priorities becomes increasingly frustrating and unsatisfying.

When you boil it down, effective leaders do two things: they think strategically to solve important problems or create new initiatives, and they develop and drive their subordinates to achieve more than they thought possible. Captain Barela, for example, was always performing both of these essential tasks. He came up with a smart strategy to fight the counterinsurgency, and he convinced his four platoon leaders that they could accomplish the mission—and held them accountable for it.

Equally important was what Captain Barela *didn't* do. He never sat around the command-and-control center all day, holding endless meetings with twenty Marines at a time to micromanage them, or even just to see how they were doing. He didn't have to, because the system of empowering small units makes those time-wasters unnecessary.

Meanwhile, the direct reports of overloaded executives become equally frustrated. They often find it hard or impossible to get face time with the boss, or even a timely reply to an email. They get stuck in their own backlog of work while waiting for feedback or decisions. This stagnation can drain any sense of empowerment—especially if the boss simultaneously insists on making key decisions rather than delegating authority. The wheels grind slower and slower, morale gets worse and worse, staff turnover accelerates, and results suffer.

Fortunately, the Marines have figured out three powerful solutions to prevent that kind of organizational stagnation. And all three worked beautifully when we migrated them to a rapidly growing business.

Strategy #1: Cap Every Team at Five Members

As Lima One grew quickly to more than two hundred employees, it often felt like we were hiring nonstop. We made a rule that whenever we hired someone to join a team that already had five members, we would split it into two teams of three each—a team leader plus two direct reports. We spelled out the division of responsibility between the two new teams, so there would be no confusion or overstepping of boundaries. The leader of each team was given authority to make as many decisions as possible within its sphere of activity.

Our goal was to give each team leader as much autonomy and responsibility as possible, pushing decisions downward instead of centralizing them upward. Capping teams at five members also allowed for streamlined decision making. "It allowed senior leaders to focus on higher-level tasks without getting bogged down with the day-to-day minutiae that comes with a larger base of direct reports," says Rankin Blair. "The structure also enabled junior employees to develop and grow quickly by being empowered to make very impactful decisions without having to wait for a higher-level approval."

Small departments contradicted conventional business wisdom. Someone with an MBA would say it's too costly and inefficient to set up two departments of three instead of a single department of six. Josh

Woodward recalls the criticism we often received: "One Wall Street investment banker actually mocked it as a 'military gimmick' and 'hokey.' I believe, though, that the small unit leadership model is integral to training and development."

Over the years we hired several people from traditional companies who tried to convince us that a flatter org chart would be better, with more direct reports per middle manager. But we rejected the entire concept of "middle management" and banned the use of that phrase at Lima One. The Marines had taught us that you manage *things*, but you lead *people*. Management is a valuable skill for organizing systems and budgeting resources, but management has nothing to do with guiding, coaching, and driving your team members. That's leadership.

So whenever we had department heads who asked for more than four direct reports, we always said no. No one, not even the CEO, was exempt from the rule of threes and fours. Anyone who didn't like this rule was free to go elsewhere. We weren't going to sacrifice the effectiveness and cohesion of Lima One just to stroke someone's ego.

Many years later, we learned that Amazon uses a similar organizational principle, which it calls the two-pizza rule:

In the early days of Amazon, Jeff Bezos instituted a rule: every internal team should be small enough that it can be fed with two pizzas. The goal wasn't to cut down on the catering bill. It was . . . focused on two aims: efficiency and scalability. The former is obvious. A smaller team spends less time managing timetables and keeping people up to date, and more time doing what needs to be done. But it's the latter that really matters for Amazon. The thing about having lots of small teams is that they all need to be able to work together, and to be able to access the common resources of the company, in order to achieve their larger goals.[*]

---

[*]   https://www.theguardian.com/technology/2018/apr/24/the-two-pizza-rule-and-the-secret-of-amazons-success.

Strategy #2: Use Commander's Intent to Push Authority Downward

Commander's intent is a powerful Marine technique that helps prevent micromanaging and instead pushes authority as far down the organization as possible. The leader's role is to explain very clearly *what* needs to be accomplished, *why* it matters, and the general scope and parameters of the mission. Once that intent has been expressed, the leader is expected to let go of *how* the goals are achieved. The subordinate is free to figure out the details.

Too many corporate bosses do the exact opposite, spelling out exactly what steps they want their subordinates to take. Then they follow up to make sure things were done exactly according to whatever they consider the "right" way. The problem is that when situations inevitably change, people need to be prepared to adapt to the unexpected. If your boss basically says, "First do step A, then step B, then step C," what happens when step A gets derailed? You may have no idea what to do, so you'll kick the problem back to the boss for further instructions.

But what if there's no time to wait for further instructions, such as during a pitch meeting with a client? Or what if your boss is away or unavailable, or just too swamped to give you timely feedback? How will you learn to think for yourself if you're never encouraged or empowered to try? How will you learn to recover from mistakes if you're never given the freedom to make them?

Commander's intent solves all those problems. As a leader, you set up guardrails for what your people can and can't do to achieve the mission, ideally making the zone between the rails as wide as possible. Within those parameters, they are free to make decisions without prior approval. They will get credit for positive outcomes and take responsibility for negative outcomes, at least those not beyond anyone's control. As long as the subordinate understands the commander's intent and takes ownership of the mission, he or she will usually rise to the occasion, even when new obstacles arise.

Here's an example of how it worked in Iraq. A squad would be assigned a patrol mission to search for reported terrorists in the area. The squad leader would be briefed on the general guidelines, such as which streets were off-limits, and under what standards it would be acceptable to open fire. But then the squad leader was free to conduct the patrol as he saw fit. He knew he'd be held responsible for the results, good or bad. If something unexpected happened, such as a problem from civilians or a sniper attack from insurgents, he was empowered to change the plan on the fly.

Imagine how bad it would be if the squad leader had to call the platoon commander for guidance whenever circumstances changed. His squad would be utterly paralyzed whenever the shit hit the fan. Instead, commander's intent protects Marines in life-or-death situations. Even if a platoon commander gets killed, his subordinates are fully prepared to continue the mission. They have the knowledge and clarity of purpose to make tough decisions under pressure.

"The Corps has a culture that produces problem solvers," says Sergeant MacGregor. "Improvise, adapt, overcome. It's built around small-unit leaders who are provided with a mission and intent and are trusted to achieve a desired outcome, without heavy-handed interference from higher-ups. We say, 'Don't stifle subordinate initiative.'"

In a corporate setting, commander's intent means that if the boss is out sick or takes a personal day, the team knows what needs to get done and has the freedom to make decisions. Likewise, the boss can take a real vacation without checking in daily, as so many neurotic managers do. She can even tell her team *not* to call or text for guidance during her vacation, no matter how much the team might be tempted to pass the buck upward.

For a boss, the only downside of commander's intent is having to give up the ego rush of making all the key decisions. It's so easy to think you're indispensable and develop an inflated sense of self-esteem in a corporate culture that narrowly restricts decision making. But in the long run, it's more satisfying to let go, watch other people develop their expertise and leadership skills, and take pride in their accomplishments. Jim Collins, in his classic book *Good to Great*, calls this Level 5 Leadership—"A powerful mixture of personal humility and indomitable will." Lesser leaders are too insecure to train their teams to shine in their absence. They need to feel irreplaceable.

One great example of commander's intent happened during a training exercise at Camp Lejeune, when JW's MEU weapons platoon was assigned the role of a TRAP (tactical recovery of aircraft personnel) force. They were charged with rescuing any downed pilots, training for weeks to handle difficult fast roping from helicopters at night. This was in January and the weather was exceptionally cold. One newly arrived Marine had been patrolling most of the afternoon and suffered from hypothermia after his first training exercise. JW decided to take him to the hospital personally, leaving the rest of the platoon behind.

Of course, if this had been actual combat, any good platoon commander would have stayed with the platoon. But since it was a training exercise, JW was more concerned about the health of his new Marine. He knew the platoon had been well trained and could handle the rest of the exercise without him. And sure enough, they did great while he was away at the hospital. They didn't need any micromanaging to adapt to changing circumstances. JW saw their success as a source of pride, not insecurity. It was proof of his own success as the platoon's leader.

For a subordinate, the only downside of commander's intent is giving up the security of not being responsible for anything. Work may feel safer if your boss gives you step-by-step instructions and makes all the decisions. But in that kind of culture, you'll never enjoy the deep satisfaction of owning the outcome and feeling trusted.

Strategy #3: Shift People Around

The Marines also build breadth of skills by rotating people around to different assignments. That's why JW was transferred from a rifle platoon to a weapons platoon after his deployment in Iraq. Even Top, who spent two decades in the infantry, was given a "transitional billet" as a stateside recruiter in 2001. He was in New York City on and after 9/11.

Along with building skills, this kind of rotation is designed to minimize "comfort and friendship." The Marines don't want leaders to become too close to their subordinates, which might cloud their judgment. It's tough to enforce a high standard if you consider your subordinate a friend. JW found that to be true near the end of his deployment in Iraq, when he was very close to his squad leaders and the other Marines under his care. That is why infantry officers and staff NCOs are usually rotated after every overseas deployment.

Job rotation is harder to do in the business world, because people are less likely to want to move to a different department after getting good at one function. But we still found ways to do some shifting at Lima One, usually in tandem with team splitting. As we divided our growing teams, we often brought in new team leaders from other departments who had no specific experience with their new department. We knew that if they had a proven skill set and a track record of mastering new challenges, they would figure it out.

For instance, at one point we created a separate team for capital markets, so we needed a head of capital markets. We chose to give that job to a team leader in rental underwriting named Clayton Barrett. He had no experience with anything related to capital markets, but he was very capable and a quick learner. Barrett stepped up to the challenge and did great. Another time we decided to split off an underwriting team, to focus on selling to clients who weren't big enough to have a face-to-face sales rep. We took a handful of good underwriters and said congratulations, you're now our inside sales department. They also rose to the challenge.

Empower Your Fireteams!

None of these organizational and leadership practices are that complicated, because they're based on how people really respond to incentives.

Micromanaging, disrespecting, and treating employees like little kids makes them demoralized and unproductive. But treating people like adults, trusting them with responsibility, and giving them latitude within clear boundaries builds enthusiasm and team spirit. Empowering leadership also helps people raise the bar and deliver their best possible work.

In Ramadi, after we mourned the tragic KIA of Corporal Tomci, Lima Company adapted. Lieutenant Sherman of Third Platoon was moved laterally to take command of Fourth Platoon, replacing the platoon commander who had frozen after the IED explosion. A staff sergeant who had been acting platoon sergeant of Third Platoon became its platoon commander for the remainder of the deployment. A squad leader in Third Platoon was promoted to platoon sergeant, two fireteam leaders were promoted to squad leaders, and two Marines became fireteam leaders to fill those vacancies. The adjustment process was fast, smooth, and natural. No single leader was indispensable, but *every* leader made a significant contribution to the overall mission.

Similarly, at Lima One, small-team leadership principles ignited a chain reaction of high standards. We set stretch goals for ourselves and our direct reports, and then they set equally high standards for their own reports, right down the line to our most junior leaders. They really did treat their departments like fireteams, with similarly great results.

How many leaders and employees in corporate America are struggling because risk-averse companies keep drawing org charts the way they've always done it, long after those charts stopped making sense? We urge you to let go of any fear of trying a new approach. A fireteam strategy will help your people become far more engaged, collaborative, and effective, beating the universal challenge of teams once and for all.

CHAPTER 7

BE BLUNT AND DIRECT

"Does This Rifle Look Clean to You?" (JW)

It was a few months before Lima Company would be shipped out to Iraq, and we were in the middle of a challenging training cycle before our deployment. The whole company had spent the week training in the field at Camp Lejeune, Monday to Friday. We slept on the ground that whole week, eating nothing but MREs (Meals, Ready to Eat), and not showering. Missions could be assigned at any time, day or night. It was tough but effective training, and a great way for me to get comfortable working with my Marines, squad leaders, and platoon sergeant. I felt a sense of accomplishment as the week drew to a close. But I was also ready for it to be over.

When we returned to our barracks Friday morning, Lima Company's executive officer, Lieutenant Clark, had some great news for me and the other three platoon commanders. "Get your platoon's weapons cleaned," he said, "and then the company will be secured." These words were music to our ears, because they meant that we'd be getting weekend liberty. We'd have two and a half days off duty, which we highly valued.

I passed the word to my platoon sergeant that everyone could take off as soon as our rifles were clean. He told the squad leaders, who quickly rounded up their squads to hit the armory. About forty-five minutes later, my platoon sergeant reported back to me, "Weapons are good to go, sir." I then passed the word up to Lieutenant Clark. We were counting the seconds until we could jump in our cars and leave base.

Unfortunately, in my excitement I had skipped one of the most crucial steps for any Marine Corps leader, which is to supervise and inspect. Because I had already cleaned my own rifle, I did not go to the armory with my Marines. Somehow, I'd forgotten a saying they taught us in OCS: "Inspect what you expect." My fellow platoon commanders were just as negligent.

While the whole company was waiting for liberty to start, Lieutenant Clark called the four platoon commanders together. He didn't raise his voice, but he ripped us for all the dirty rifles he had just inspected in the armory. One of his *least* critical comments was, "Those were the nastiest weapons I've ever seen in my life." You can imagine the rest. Most of the company had obviously rushed through and half-assed the cleaning, creating a serious hazard for the next time those rifles would be used. But Lieutenant Clark didn't blame the enlisted men—he correctly blamed the four of us for not supervising our platoons. He reminded us that it was our responsibility to uphold high standards. When he added, "I would fire every one of you if I were your CO!" I felt my stomach sink. How was I going to tell people that I got canned from my first command before we even deployed to Iraq?

"Any questions?" he concluded.

None of us had any questions. And we certainly weren't going to blame our platoon sergeants, squad leaders, or Marines. Ultimately, it was our failure. All we could do was absorb the criticism, accept responsibility, and go fix the problem.

We started by each talking to our platoon sergeants and squad leaders in private, then accompanying our platoons back to the armory. After every rifle was taken apart again, I ran a Q-tip along one of the barrels. As the Q-tip turned black, I held it up to the Marine in front of me. "Does this rifle look clean to you?"

The only possible reply: "No, sir."

I did the same to four or five additional weapons, with each Q-tip turning a nasty, gritty black. Everyone was embarrassed, and not another word needed to be said. The platoon kept working in the armory until every rifle was spotless. Only then was the company secured for the weekend.

But before I could get to my car, the four platoon commanders were summoned once again by Lieutenant Clark. Apparently, he wasn't done with us yet. As we walked to his office, different types of cruel punishment rushed through my mind. At Infantry Officer Course, I'd been forced to paint the entranceway one weekend for an infraction. The worst thing imaginable would be if he named me officer of the day on Saturday—a twenty-four-hour posting in the battalion headquarters from 7:00 a.m. to 7:00 a.m. That would have killed the whole weekend.

As we entered his office, Lieutenant Clark rose and asked a question that completely shocked me: "All right, who wants to drive to the O-Club [officers' club] for lunch? I could use a good buffet right now." Earlier he had wanted to fire us, but now he wanted to have lunch with us? While my head was still spinning, we all hopped in my car and went to lunch, where not another word was spoken about the rifles.

Out of all of my Marine Corps experiences, this one may have had the biggest impact on my future behavior, in business and in life. I am eternally grateful for Lieutenant Clark's leadership and mentoring, and the example he set. As our superior, he asked the four of us to accomplish an important task. We failed at that task. He immediately held us accountable, but in a professional way. He made sure that we corrected the situation. Perhaps most impressively, he didn't hold a grudge against us. Once the matter was resolved, there was no need to ever mention it again.

For the rest of my time with Lima Company, we never had another problem with dirty rifles. Seventeen years later, Lieutenant Clark still needles me about the incident: "Before Ramadi, you guys couldn't even clean your weapons."

The Age of the Feedback Sandwich

At some point in the last few decades, American society became allergic to straight talk, especially in the context of evaluating and leading people. Too many people became conflict-averse and two-faced. We're not sure exactly why, but instead of leaders simply telling subordinates what they were doing right and wrong, they started soft-pedaling their feedback. Almost like the parents of little kids, leaders started looking for any excuse to say something positive, while they cushioned even the slightest negative feedback with positive context.

Old-school tough bosses, the kind who routinely screamed, threw tantrums, and fired people on a whim, were forced to reform their ways, and rightly so. If they couldn't or wouldn't reform, many were driven out of big companies. But those positive developments often went too far in the other direction. Newer bosses began to hold back from pointing out mistakes altogether, unless those mistakes were truly mission critical. Annual performance reviews became increasingly filled with happy talk and euphemisms. Unacceptable work was relabeled with terms like "opportunities for growth and development." The new goal, apparently, was to prevent demoralization of the workforce via overly harsh criticism.

One common management strategy promoted by HR professionals was the feedback sandwich. Department heads were taught that if they wanted to correct one of their direct reports, they had to start with a positive statement. Then slip in the constructive criticism, phrased as gently as possible. Then finish with another slice of positive bread, praising the employee for something else they were doing well. We assume many managers loved this tactic because it made them feel less guilty about pointing out mistakes. Maybe they started to see their direct reports as delicate flowers who would wither under the slightest criticism.

But the feedback sandwich and similar tactics often backfire, because most people can tell when their superiors are being condescending or insincere. Unless a boss is an exceptionally good actor, any praise-criticism-praise conversation comes off as phony and even disrespectful. Instead of feeling better about their workplace and inspired to improve their shortcomings, many people leave that kind of conversation feeling worse. We've heard stories of workers who quickly forgot the praise but were haunted by the criticism, wondering where they really stood and what the boss might not be telling them. Instead of learning anything, they felt confused. *Is he happy with me or upset? Is my job in jeopardy? Do they think I'm performing well?* Nothing is worse than having to guess where you stand.

The Best Strategy: Blunt and Direct

The Marines teach that the best way to communicate in any situation is simple: direct, blunt, immediate feedback, with neither positive nor negative emotions getting in the way of constructive criticism. The Marine guideline was simple: Make it CLEAR, CONCISE, and COMPELLING.

If you screw up in the Marines, you will be told exactly what you did wrong and what you need to do differently, as soon your leader notices. The sooner the feedback follows the incident in question, the more impact it has. Then it's over and you can move forward. You know what you have to fix and, equally important, you don't have to wonder where you stand.

Starting from day one of our Marine training, we both experienced extremely blunt communication from our leaders. Some examples of how it was framed:

Do this, don't do that.

You're doing it the wrong way, watch how I do it the right way.

That's not good enough, go back and try again.

You failed to accomplish your mission.

You're below average among your peers because . . .

Here are three reasons you're not getting promoted . . .

Civilians might see this kind of communication as disrespectful, but we actually found it very respectful. Telling someone exactly what you expect from them, and how they're measuring up to those expectations, is a sign that you value them enough not to bullshit them. It signals that if something is wrong, you as a leader will make the effort to speak up immediately. And if your criticism comes across as fair and reasonable, the recipient will hopefully not interpret it as a personal attack.

Conversely, whenever we were praised by our leaders, we knew it was sincere. They wouldn't say anything positive unless we earned it, just as they wouldn't waste time ragging on us unless we deserved the criticism. No mind games in either direction. Unlike elementary school soccer teams, the Marines don't do participation trophies.

When we started to grow the staff at Lima One Capital, we resolved to follow the Marine Corps model of communication, rather than the corporate HR model. That gave us a big competitive advantage in developing and retaining talent, as you'll see in the rest of this chapter. "The company was growing rapidly and there often wasn't time for pleasantries or long debates," remembers Rankin Blair. "The success or failure of the company depended on acting quickly to seize opportunities. The direct communication cut through all the noise of the moment and helped keep everyone moving in the same direction." We've continued the same tactics at GEM Mining.

As effective as this approach is, it can initially intimidate those who tend to be quiet and nonconfrontational, as well as any employees who have never experienced blunt feedback from their parents, teachers, coaches, or previous bosses. But once they get used to it, most people find it totally refreshing. Sooner or later, they realize that direct feedback is much better than fuzzy expectations, awkward silences, and ambiguous performance reviews. It's also far better than the other extreme, a culture of screaming, taunting, and public humiliation that terrorizes people into blind obedience. Josh Woodward summarizes this result:

> The blunt and direct form of communication bred authenticity internally and externally—it backboned our culture. Even if the communication was unfavorable, it created a tremendous amount of clarity, which created comfort and confidence for us to perform better. I'd rather know that I have things to improve upon than be doing a great job and not know where I stand. Blunt and direct communication increased our individual and collective self-awareness. Externally, we were perceived as being different. When most company leaders tended to hold back or be coy in business conversations, our contrast of getting to the point and bluntly telling people (clients, banks, investors, etc.) how we felt, positively or negatively, has a resonating impact. We gained immediate respect.

We've even found that being blunt and direct works best in personal relationships. In a rigorous scientific survey (sample size: two marriages), we've found that 90 percent of spousal arguments stem from miscommunication about expectations or intentions. If you practice being blunt and direct with your loved ones and encourage them to be blunt and direct about their desires and assumptions, you can resolve most issues before they escalate to serious conflict. How many relationships, both professional and personal, are wrecked because people bottle up their frustrations instead of dealing with them, respectfully but directly?

Another great example is in dealing with children. Do you realize that no other group of people are more blunt than kids? They don't know a tactful way of communicating, so they just come right out and say whatever they're thinking. And they appreciate the same, more than most parents realize. For instance, JW recently watched his six-year-old's soccer team get totally shellacked by their opponents. After the game,

JW told his son, "I was proud of how hard you played, even when you were down ten to nothing. That took real heart."

Stevie replied, "Thanks, Dad. I'm glad you didn't say, 'Good game!' It wasn't a good game—we got killed!"

Stressing Facts, Downplaying Emotions

When communicating bluntly, one should always stay unemotional and respectful. The dirty-rifles incident made such an impression on JW because Lieutenant Clark's criticism was factual, not emotional. Maybe he really was angry at his platoon leaders, but he didn't attack us personally. He focused on the two critical lessons, about proper weapons maintenance and proper supervision of our platoons. Then the feedback was over, and we all moved on with no lingering resentments. We were able to continue socializing with Lieutenant Clark off duty, because none of us took it personally. The point was education, not retribution.

We all knew that Lieutenant Clark was a great leader and mentor. He clearly cared about his platoon commanders and wanted us to succeed. "I looked at Clark as the person who taught me how to be an officer," recalled Lieutenant Sherman. But he was never going to put his feelings for us—neither his friendship nor his occasional anger—ahead of our mission or the safety of every single Marine in the company. "Leadership should never be personal, but a lot of people get personal," Lieutenant Clark once said.

Strong emotions, both positive and negative, can be extremely dangerous in any leadership situation. If you lose your temper with a subordinate, you can apologize and they might forgive you, but they won't forget it. They will start to think of you as someone who flies off the handle and can't stay cool under stress. That hurts your credibility as a leader, and it can destroy your moral authority if a pattern of yelling continues. Anger is corrosive, not constructive, especially when vented in public, in front of the target's peers or subordinates.

Brandy Cogsdill, who headed up Lima One's loan servicing department, says that she is most proud of the company's authenticity, which wasn't common in the business world. "Good or bad," she notes, "you knew where you stood and what needed to be done. I appreciated the transparency. Also, I was never spoken to in any way that was not respectful."

Many leaders go to the other extreme from the screamers, holding back negative emotions but showing lots of warmth, friendship, and emotional support. This style is more popular with subordinates in the short run, because everyone loves positive feedback. But it's equally damaging to morale and effectiveness in the long run.

Imagine if Lieutenant Clark had tried a feedback sandwich, praising us for our performance during the training before slipping in a few words about the dirty rifles. Or imagine if he had said something like, "Hey, guys, I checked the armory, and the rifles look kinda dirty. But don't worry about it this time—I don't want to delay your liberty. Next time just please supervise the cleaning more closely. Enjoy your weekend!" Either way, I suspect the four of us would have forgotten that feedback in an hour, and the company's overall standard of excellence would have taken a serious hit.

The Art of the Performance Review

In addition to getting instant feedback after every instance of substandard behavior, every Marine gets a monthly fitness review. The goal is to make sure you know exactly how well you're doing relative to your peer group and the expectations for your rank. These reviews can be very brief if nearly everything is on track. *Here's where you're meeting or exceeding expectations. Here's where you're falling below expectations. Here's what you need to focus on this month. Any questions?*

A Marine's progress goals are clear and unambiguous. For instance, suppose you're a private and you want to get promoted to lance corporal. You have a detailed checklist of accomplishments and qualifications required for promotion. This way, you and your squad leader are reading from the same playbook. The review metrics are specific. What's your score on the physical fitness test? How accurate is your marksmanship on the firing range? Are you caught up on the correspondence classes you're required to do while off duty?

When you have enough seniority to be considered for promotion, your proficiency and conduct metrics from all those monthly reviews are right there in your file. You shouldn't be surprised by your unit's decision about whether you get promoted or not. If you haven't been improving from month to month, you already know what the answer will be.

In contrast, the typical performance review in corporate America is far less straightforward. It's usually annual or at best semiannual, so your last review may be a distant memory. Problems can easily fall through the cracks between official reviews if the boss isn't good at giving consistent feedback. The categories of evaluation are often vague, like attendance and punctuality. Is anyone measuring how often you came in late or handed in your deliverables later than agreed to? If not, how are you supposed to know if you're improving? This is why so many people get blindsided by bad performance reviews, walking into them with no clue that the boss has any major concerns. In that situation, the shock can feel worse than the criticism.

As Lima One began to expand, we resolved to do feedback and reviews the Marine Corps way. We expected our department heads to comment immediately on any substandard behavior, and to do *monthly* one-on-one performance reviews. All feedback had to be specific and fact-based. *You did X, next time do Y instead.* No one ever had to wonder where they stood, what they needed to do to get promoted, or how to save their jobs if they were in trouble.

We found that employees appreciated this approach. "Personally, I preferred the blunt directness provided by John and Top," says Drew Fitzpatrick. "This kind of communication allowed for both personal and professional growth; even if the communication was more constructive, the transparency was one of the most valuable components."

Katie Summersett echoes those sentiments: "I appreciated it. I always knew where I stood, and it helped me be the best version of myself."

We taught department heads that it was just as important to make positive feedback blunt, direct, and consistent. Why wait a month or longer to recognize someone for doing a great job? Our rule was to speak up whenever you notice someone doing outstanding work. *I was really impressed when you did X—keep doing that.* Instant praise is just as powerful as instant correction. Then a note could go into the file for the next monthly review.

Blunt and direct communication also minimizes the typical office politics that can infect organizations. "When I reported to John, I always knew where I stood with him and the company," recalls Justin Thompson. "My colleagues always knew where they stood with me, and I with them. I remember that time as being remarkably free of office politics and palace intrigue."

The Art of the Group Presentation

The same strategies apply to group communications, whether you're explaining an idea to a chow hall full of Marines or a boardroom full of Wall Street investors. Regardless of how smart and sophisticated your audience is, it's always better to be as clear, concise, and compelling as possible. A lot of businesspeople fall into the trap of trying to make their presentations too complex. They create long, dense pitch decks in a misguided attempt to look smarter. If they're given a time block of thirty minutes, they plan to use every second of it.

But even if you're presenting to Bill Gates or Elon Musk, you will be far more successful by keeping your points simple. Do you really need ten bullets on a slide if only three are truly important? Does that chart or graph make your message clearer or more confusing? If you only talk for eighteen minutes instead of thirty, do you think your audience will feel disappointed that you got to the Q&A faster?

Of course, it's harder and takes longer to prepare clear-concise-compelling presentations rather than everything-but-the-kitchen-sink presentations. It forces you to weed out excessive complexity and irrelevant information, draft after draft. You may also have to get past your own insecurity—your desire to prove how much you know and how much homework you've done.

The most successful leaders come up with simple answers to complex problems, and then figure out how to communicate those answers just as simply. If you read or watch videos of outstanding speeches, from Abraham Lincoln to Winston Churchill to Martin Luther King Jr. to today's most popular TED Talk presenters, you'll see the common thread of "clear, concise, and compelling."

Address the Four Brain Quadrants (JW)

My friend Mike Morris, a consultant and a great communicator, once gave me some powerful feedback on my first presentation to potential investors. He drew a two-by-two table and labeled the four resulting boxes: Strategic, Data/Numbers, Operations, Emotion. "These are the four brain quadrants that every human uses to make decisions. In every presentation, pitch, or persuasion effort, all four quadrants need to be addressed."

He added that all of us are dominated by one or at most two of these quadrants. "John, your pitch primarily focused on operations, on your plan to accomplish the mission. You also addressed some data and numbers. But you totally failed to say anything about the strategic vision of the company, and your pitch had zero emotional pull."

Mike's diagram and advice changed my career forever. Ever since, I've forced myself to address all four quadrants in every kind of communication. In addition to talking about Lima One's operations, I got emotional about the positive impact our borrowers and our loans had on communities. I showed before-and-after photos of projects we had financed. I spent more time on the company's long-term vision.

When filled with blunt and direct communication, those four boxes became a road map for raising billions of dollars.

Blunt Communication Promotes Meritocracy

At Lima One, we publicly recognized outstanding performance at our company-wide monthly meetings, announcing the top performers in various departments, such as sales, underwriting, loan servicing, and construction. People like to know who the high performers are, and they like to know that if they ever achieve at a similar level, they will also get to enjoy public praise from senior management.

This aspect of blunt communication helped us run Lima One as a meritocracy, minimizing favoritism. We never saw anyone who failed to get public praise become bitter or disgruntled, because the folks we recognized had the metrics to back up their recognition. Everything was transparent— for instance, how many loan applications did they process that month? How many loans did they close? How did those loans perform? How many borrowers defaulted?

In many organizations, ambiguous standards and superficial performance reviews create a huge temptation for bosses to play favorites. Suppose you've got five direct reports and one of them is your not-so-secret favorite. Maybe the two of you are personal friends outside work, or you went to the same college or attend the same church. When your favorite blows a few deadlines, you just shrug it off. But when your least favorite employee blows a few deadlines, you come down on them hard. Favoritism doesn't merely kill your relationship with that one disfavored person—it signals to everyone that you're not a straight shooter. That kills your credibility. Clear communication increases meritocracy, meritocracy reduces jealousy, and low levels of jealousy reduce turnover.

Blunt Communication Improves Bad Situations (JW)

We don't want to give the impression that we expected perfection from everyone at all times. That would be insanely unrealistic. We told people that everyone screws up, but the test of your character is what you do about it. We expected blunt and direct communication even when that meant admitting something they'd rather avoid discussing. If something goes wrong, speak up immediately. Waiting just introduces unnecessary additional stress and makes the situation worse.

I learned this crucial lesson during one of my worst moments at Officer Candidates School. It was about a week before OCS graduation, and we had just come back to barracks from our final field exercises. We were coated in mud and exhausted after a full week in the field, but we felt a huge sense of accomplishment. We had reached the unofficial stage of OCS where the motto was, *Don't do anything stupid and you'll be a Marine officer!* I had no idea how close I would come to not making it.

Before we could go into the barracks, we needed to take outdoor showers to get all that mud off us. We leaned our rifles up against the wall outside the showers, as we had done numerous times. When I finished cleaning up, I went to grab my rifle, but it was gone. Everyone else's rifles were right where they had left them, but mine had vanished without a trace.

This was a huge problem, because it's a major rule in the Marine Corps that you never leave your weapon out of reach, or at least out of sight. I felt a wave of gut-churning terror. Losing a rifle could result in the shutdown of the entire base. Careers could be ruined all the way up the chain of command for such an offense. On top of all that, I was left with a sickening thought: *I'm going to have to tell everyone I got kicked out of OCS with a week left because I lost my rifle!*

For a minute or so I was too stunned to do anything. Then I realized that there was only one valid option. I walked into the barracks, to the small office of my platoon sergeant, Gunnery Sergeant Casarez.

"Request permission to talk to the platoon sergeant."

He looked up at me, stone-faced. "Granted. What is it?"

"This candidate has lost his rifle."

To this day, those were the hardest words I've ever had to say. Shame and embarrassment flooded my body. I went on to explain that I'd put my rifle down while showering and it was missing afterward. "I have no idea what happened to it, Gunnery Sergeant."

He paused for a few long seconds to stare at me. Then he reached under his desk and pulled out a rifle. "Is this your weapon?" I saw the white athletic tape wrapped around the buttstock, with handwritten letters on it: "W-A-R-R-E-N."

I now realized that this had been yet another test. But did I pass or fail? Would I graduate from OCS or be on the next Greyhound bus back to South Carolina?

Gunnery Sergeant Casarez reamed me out for leaving my rifle outside my reach. Then he added, "I want you to know that if you hadn't owned up to this immediately, we would have kicked your ass out of the Marine Corps." It wouldn't have mattered if I had lied or merely tried to hide what happened, because a lie of omission is still a lie. But because I owned up to the mistake, I would get to graduate and become a Marine. My only punishment was having to do guard duty for the final weekend, which meant no visiting M Street in Washington, DC, with my buddies.

Remember the scandal of the so-called London Whale? In 2012 a trader for JPMorgan Chase made some terrible bets and wound up deep in the red in his trading account. But instead of telling his bosses and asking for help, he hid his mistakes and kept making bigger and bigger bets to try to undo his losses. He wound up losing about $6 billion of the company's money, a catastrophe that led to new government regulations. Every day in the corporate world, someone else is doing the same on a smaller scale— making problems worse by not communicating bluntly and immediately.

At Lima One people came to us quickly whenever problems arose because of our zero-tolerance policy for lying, including lies of omission. Bringing a possible solution to the problem was even better. We may not have always agreed with that proposed solution, but we respected anyone who put in the effort. Part of accountability is trying to clean up your own messes, not dumping them into someone else's lap.

Blunt Communication and Accountability
with External Partners

We taught our employees to use blunt and direct communication with people outside Lima One as well as inside. If they wanted to work with us, our vendors, appraisers, property inspectors, lawyers, and even our investors would have to get used to clearly expressed expectations and mutually agreed-upon standards. *We both agree that you're doing X and we're doing Y, by these dates. Right?* We expected our partners to be deadline-driven, and we made it clear that we would keep track of those deadlines. Then if a deadline was blown, we would refer to our agreement. We often used the line, "We aren't being unreasonable. We're simply holding you accountable to your original commitment."

Many found this approach very different from what they routinely experienced with other organizations. Often, those on the receiving end of that comment were utterly shocked that someone had actually held them accountable. We've found that one of two things will happen when you confront external partners with blunt accountability. Some will quickly recognize that they need to uphold the highest standards in dealing with you, because you take accountability seriously. They may elevate their game relative to how they treat other organizations. And if they have open minds, they may come to agree that clarity and accountability are better than ambiguity and vague standards.

The other category of external partners will resist accountability. They'll come up with excuses as to why their prior commitments should no longer apply and why they won't live up to mutually agreed standards. That's when things can get tricky.

In 2017 we made a deal with a wholly owned subsidiary of a famous investment firm that managed more than $100 billion in capital. Let's call it Acme. We negotiated an agreement with them to purchase a large portfolio of our fix-and-flip loans, with Lima One servicing them. It was a clear, concise agreement. But immediately upon closing that agreement, when we sent Acme their first batch of roughly $8 million in loans, they began to cherry-pick the loans, refusing to take some of them, which was a clear violation of our deal.

Reneging on an agreement to buy a loan, aka "retrading," is a significant offense in our industry. It created problems for our other investors, who effectively would get stuck with the loans the cherry picker didn't want. That hurt our reputation and threatened our overall business. We pushed back against Acme, bluntly and directly. "That wasn't the plan that we agreed to. You can't just retrade any loans that you've now changed your mind about."

Apparently, they thought they could push us around and take advantage of us, because they were larger and more prestigious than we were. Acme's response was extremely disrespectful. They questioned everything we were doing and insisted that they had the right to cherry-pick our loans. They also challenged the servicing fees we charged on the loans they did buy, which had also been spelled out in our agreement.

Eventually, we made the tough decision to cut Acme off from about $50 million in additional loans that we had originated and planned to sell to the firm. For us this was a line-in-the-sand moment. We refused to tolerate dishonorable and unethical behavior, no matter who the counter party; a deal is a deal. How could we talk to our own people about accountability with a straight face if we didn't hold Acme accountable?

By canceling the rest of our loan sales, we made things very difficult for Acme, which had been set up specifically to buy our kind of loans. They came back to us with an apology and a vague promise to do better. They even sent a team from New York down to our office in Greenville, trying to resell us and reinstate our deal. But at that point, after so much dishonesty, it was too late. They had blown their credibility.

The CEO of Acme got fired, and soon after, Acme was dissolved, put out of business by its parent company. We moved forward with other partners who aligned with our standards of integrity.

The Power of Sharing Information (JW)

Blunt and direct communication is more than a tool for evaluating, rewarding, and punishing individuals. It's also an essential tool for bonding an entire organization together, through the power of sharing information.

As with so many of our leadership tactics, we learned this one from Captain Barela. Unlike most company commanders, he held meetings for the full company every two weeks, in the chow hall at Snakepit. Everyone came, down to the privates, except for a couple of squads on duty guarding the perimeter of the base. Captain Barela gave us a full update on what was going on in our sector. Operations that were going well, or not going so well. Plans for future operations. Whatever he was hearing from the battalion command. Those meetings were exceptionally open and honest, sharing much more detail than other companies. It made everyone feel included and respected. They were always followed by a question-and-answer segment where no question was out of bounds.

First Platoon did something similar when we started developing intelligence from local civilians. Sometimes I'd have a long meeting with a source, from thirty minutes to two hours, with just a radio operator and an interpreter, frantically writing down information as the source talked. When we got back to base at the end of the night, the rest of the platoon wanted to know what happened. Every night, I stayed up to type my scribbled notes, while they were still fresh in my mind. Then I'd give the debrief to the squad leaders and tell them what we learned, with orders to spread this confidential intelligence to the entire platoon. I wanted them to know I respected and valued their role in the mission, even though they weren't in the room with the source. We were a true team, each of us fulfilling vital roles to accomplish our shared mission.

I also made sure not to sugarcoat any of the debriefs. Sometimes they'd say that we wasted two hours and got zero actionable information. People appreciated the honesty even when they were disappointed by the results. They'd rather hear, "We got nothing tonight, but we appreciate you providing security. Hopefully the next source will give us more." That was much better than leaving them to wonder about the results and thinking that I didn't care enough to update them. Hiding key information kills morale and stirs up rumors that are usually worse than whatever bad news a leader is hiding.

At Lima One we used the same methods to communicate key information down to the lowest level of the organization. We shared many confidential details that would normally be kept from most employees, starting literally on day one, when we presented the full investor briefing that we described in Chapter 5. We told them that this financial data was proprietary and not to be shared with outsiders—but now they were insiders, so we trusted them.

Every quarter we held a full company meeting, modeled after Captain Barela's talks in the Snakepit chow hall. We distributed and explained a summary of Lima One's financial results for the previous quarter, such as how many new loans originated, how many paid off or defaulted, and how much capital we had in reserve. We also took time to praise the best individual performers of the previous quarter. We now do the same at GEM Mining—here's how many new mining machines became operational, how much Bitcoin we produced, and so on.

This kind of transparency is especially valuable when the news isn't great. If you tell your people, "We had a tough quarter," but you don't give any details, or any hint of how your strategy will change, what do you expect them to think? How can they help you solve big problems if you don't help them understand those problems? The situation is far worse when you don't even admit you had a bad quarter.

Most corporate cultures default to secrecy because knowledge is power, and poor leaders care more about preserving their power than about empowering their teams. If you can let go of that flawed mindset, transparency can turbocharge organizational effectiveness. The more you keep proving to your employees that you really do care about them and respect them, the more they will outperform expectations.

The Fork in the Road

We live in an age of euphemism and indirectness. Sometimes it seems like everyone from politicians to doctors to the media has forgotten how to give straight answers to simple questions. Corporate leaders are among the worst offenders.

Blunt and direct communication provides so many benefits. Eliminating ambiguous standards means there's less cover for favoritism or aimless leadership. Requiring immediate ownership of mistakes prevents problems from snowballing and builds accountability. Refusing to tolerate duplicitous partners may seem to hurt in the short run but always pays off in the long run. Being transparent with your employees may reduce your exclusive hold on key knowledge, but it helps maintain an empowered team of killers.

The common thread of all the situations in this chapter—from performance reviews to confronting outside partners to sharing financial details—is that in each case a leader faces a fork in the road. On one side is the road to vague happy talk, silence, ambiguity, or outright lying. On the other side is the road to clarity, facts, specific details, and blunt honesty.

The path you choose will make all the difference.

CHAPTER 8

ENFORCE UP-OR-OUT

Up-or-Out in the Marines

Marines often observe that the Corps gets easier after you get through boot camp or Officer Candidates School. If you consistently show up on time, stay physically fit, do your job, and meet your requirements for ongoing training and education, you'll probably get promoted on or close to the standard schedule. At your quarterly or annual fitness reviews, depending on your rank, your commander will let you know where you're measuring up or falling short, as we saw in the chapter on blunt feedback.

But there will always be some Marines who can't keep up with the minimum requirements, and who don't respond to feedback on how to improve. In those cases, the principle that kicks in is "up-or-out." You have a certain window of time to prove that you've mastered your current responsibilities and have earned a promotion to the next higher rank. If you can't or won't do what's required within that time frame, you will be pushed out. The Corps isn't going to allow you to just stick around without improving. They want you to be constantly improving and moving forward in your career, or else they'd rather process you out, so you won't be a drag on your unit.

The technical term for these windows of opportunity is "service limitations." For the junior enlisted ranks—private, private first class (PFC), and lance corporal—you have the remainder of your four-year commitment to get promoted. For the higher enlisted ranks, the windows are much longer—especially since they were lengthened somewhat in 2018. The current service limitations are:

- Corporal: 8 years
- Sergeant: 12 years
- Staff sergeant: 20 years
- Gunnery sergeant: 22 years
- First sergeant or master sergeant: 27 years
- Sergeant major or master gunnery sergeant: 30 years[*]

But these official limits are misleading. No Marine company is going to allow a subpar corporal to stick around for eight years, or a struggling sergeant for twelve years. If they get passed over for promotion twice and are showing no signs of improvement, they will be pushed out. The same is true for officers who stall out on their development.

Other military services don't have this kind of strict commitment to up-or-out. For instance, Top recalls a joint exercise he once conducted in Australia with the British Royal Marines:

> I was twenty-three at the time and already a sergeant. My British counterpart for the joint exercise was also a sergeant, but he was forty-one and had been in the service for more than twenty years. It felt strange that this much older guy was the same rank as me,

---

[*] "Marine Corps Introduces New Service Limits," FEDWeek, December 21, 2018, https://www.fedweek.com/armed-forces-news/marine-corps-introduces-new -service-limits/.

with the same responsibilities. I got to spend a fair amount of time with him, and he was perfectly happy staying a sergeant for the long haul. This unit of the British military had no problem with a twenty-year or even twenty-five-year sergeant staying in the same role. That really struck me because the mentality was completely different from the US Marine Corps.

"Up" Means Opportunities to Give Rapid Promotions (JW)

By combining the principles of empowering fireteams and enforcing up-or-out, the Marines enable young people to earn recognition and additional responsibilities quickly. While there are often exceptions, a solid new Marine might be promoted from private to PFC in just a few months, and then to lance corporal about a year later. By that point he may be ready to lead a fireteam, with potentially life-or-death responsibility for three other Marines. This rapid rise to leadership might be scary, but it's much more inspiring than a private sector bureaucracy where there's no hope of getting promoted for years. It's one reason why the average twenty-two-year-old Marine seems more mature than the average twenty-two-year-old in the business world.

I took the principle of "promote good people quickly" very seriously. After I returned from Ramadi, I was reassigned to be a platoon commander for our battalion's weapons company, which was training at Camp Lejeune before its next deployment on a Marine Expeditionary Unit (MEU). Weapons platoons are larger than infantry platoons, with two sections normally led by staff sergeants, and three squads per section, each usually led by a sergeant. When a section leader slot opened up in my platoon, there were two sergeants eligible for the job, but I found them both mediocre at best. So instead, I gave the section leader job to an outstanding corporal.

This was an unconventional decision, but I figured that if I had a son in combat, I would much rather have him led by an excellent corporal than by a mediocre sergeant. I then moved the two sergeants over to the other section to be squad leaders, reporting to a staff sergeant as their section leader. I heard some grumbling about these unorthodox, merit-over-seniority moves from outside the platoon, but our platoon understood that they were consistent with Marine Corps values. Fortunately, I had credibility with my new platoon after my combat experience in Iraq, and the staff changes worked out well.

"Out" Can Be Easier Said than Done (JW)

It's easy to talk about up-or-out, and it can be satisfying to promote good people, but practicing the "out" part is harder. I learned that when I first joined Lima Company and took over First Platoon, before our deployment to Ramadi.

I found that my Marines were very capable as warriors and had excelled at the battle for Fallujah. On the other hand, they needed more discipline, because they had previously been led by a weak pla-toon commander who ultimately gave up command of the platoon to his strong-willed platoon sergeant. Both of them were now gone, and I was left with two squad leaders who thought no rules applied to them or their squads.

In one training exercise, for example, my squad leaders thought it would be funny to slip into another platoon's sleeping area and take many of their rifles. I tried to get them to stop cutting corners and clean up their act, but they had picked up a lot of bad habits and showed no sign of improving. I did not, and still don't, blame those squad leaders for their rebellious ways. I would have acted in the same manner if the roles were reversed. The question now was how to solve this serious problem.

I couldn't literally fire those squad leaders, but I got permission to have them reassigned. One was shipped off to another platoon and the other was demoted to fireteam leader. We replaced them with two fireteam leaders from within the company, promoting them to be squad leaders for First Platoon. Those moves sent a dramatic message to the rest of the platoon and the entire company. Although initially difficult, the transition was positive for all the Marines involved. First Platoon became more disciplined and mission-focused. My squad leader who was sent to Third Platoon excelled in Ramadi and became well respected. The other squad leader, following demotion, became one of my platoon's best fireteam leaders in Ramadi. We remain close friends to this day.

Sometimes forcing someone out is more straightforward. A few months later, during our deployment to Ramadi, I started having chronic problems with my platoon sergeant. One day he was leading a section on patrol in Humvees, while the rest of us were on foot. They were supposed to be protecting us, but when I called his radio, all I could hear was music. I found out later that he had outfitted his Humvee with speakers, and his radio headset got stuck in the engaged position, which prevented incoming communications. Not only was he distracted by listening to music while he was supposed to be providing security, but his jammed radio put the whole platoon in harm's way. That was the last straw for me, after a series of inappropriate actions. I wanted to have him removed from his billet, and Captain Barela agreed, but our battalion commander rejected that punishment as too severe.

Instead, I stripped away all of the platoon sergeant's tactical authority. He could still give administrative orders about issues like supplies, but all tactical commands now would come from me and the squad leaders. I also confined the platoon sergeant to stay inside Snakepit or OPVA. The punishment was not meant to be humiliating, simply practical. Even though this punishment didn't end his Marine career, it sent a strong and unambiguous message to the whole company that integrity, always doing the right thing, was important and would be enforced.

Decisions that will change the course of someone else's career are hard to make, and often gut-wrenching. We never took them lightly. In these situations, it is much easier to ignore problems and hope they go away on their own, rather than have a hard conversation or fire the individual. But these problems almost never resolve themselves. A lack of discipline gets worse, performance decreases, and morale plummets. As Lieutenant Clark once told me about this difficult aspect of leadership, "We took on a responsibility to lead Marines. You have to separate doing the right thing from your feelings about how uncomfortable it feels to tell somebody they've screwed up." As he and all good Marines understand, leaders must act for the good of the overall unit and make the necessary changes. If they can't or choose not to, they have failed at their most basic duty, and every one of their subordinates will know it.

Adapting Up-or-Out for Business: Jim Collins's Bus

When we adapted some of the other Marine principles for the business world, we had to make them softer in a civilian context. But in the case of up-or-out, we made a Marine practice even tougher. We created short timelines for new employees at Lima One, with tight windows for under-performers to meet the company's standards. We made it clear from the first day of onboarding that someone's career progress would be all about performance, not seniority. Even less than the Marines, Lima One couldn't afford the luxury of long "service limitations" in our fast-moving industry.

Our approach was inspired not only by the Marines but also by Jim Collins, the acclaimed author of *Good to Great* and other studies of en-during great companies. His metaphor is that a leader's most important responsibility is getting the right people on the bus, and in the right seats, and getting the wrong people off the bus. If you fail at that process, nothing else you do will matter much. As Collins wrote:

> The good-to-great leaders understood three simple truths. First, if you begin with "who" rather than "what" you can more easily adapt to a changing world. If people join the bus primarily because of where it is going, what happens if you get ten miles down the road and you need to change direction? You've got a problem. But if people are on the bus because of who else is on the bus, then it's much easier to change direction. . . . Second, if you have the right people on

the bus, the problem of how to motivate and manage people largely goes away. The right people don't need to be tightly managed or fired up; they will be self-motivated by the inner drive to produce the best results and to be part of creating something great. Third, if you have the wrong people, it doesn't matter whether you discover the right direction; you still won't have a great company.*

Our guiding principle at Lima One was "on the bus slowly but off the bus quickly." As we discussed in Chapter 4, our interview process and reference checks usually screened out people who would be a bad fit for our bus. But it wasn't foolproof, just as the Marine recruiting process wasn't perfect. If you have, say, a 95 percent success rate in recruiting a Corps of 180,000, that's 9,000 bad Marines who will make it through the filter. Even in a 200-person company, 95 percent hiring success means 10 bad apples who might poison the culture for everyone else. That's why getting the wrong people off the bus is just as important as getting the right people on.

The Power of Rapid Promotions

On a surface level, promotions are just a way to put people in more appropriate seats on the bus. If someone is qualified to do higher-level work, the organization benefits from giving them a new role to do that work. That part is obvious.

Less obvious is the psychological effect of rapid, merit-based promotions. It's a fundamental truth of human nature that public recognition really matters to people, often more than money. A raise without a promotion might make some difference to your lifestyle, but a promotion that elevates your responsibility makes you feel better about yourself and your employer. This seems to be especially true for millennials

---

*   "First Who, Then What," Jim Collins, n.d., https://www.jimcollins.com /concepts/first-who-then-what.html.

and Generation Z. We found that most of Lima One's younger staffers would rather have a small raise plus a promotion rather than a bigger raise without any career progress.

Merit has to be the sole reason for fast promotions, rather than seniority or likability or fitting into the corporate mold. Try to focus on appropriate metrics that can be clearly communicated. For instance, we judged underwriters on how many loans they were originating monthly, as well as how those loans were performing. No one could game the system by approving bad loans to underqualified borrowers. If you pick the right metrics and make them transparent, it will be clear why someone got promoted quickly over his or her peers, and you can avoid whispers about favoritism.

We hated the fact that at most companies people get promoted for seniority rather than objectively measured performance. Nothing kills morale among high performers faster than seeing someone clearly mediocre get promoted ahead of you, just because they have an extra year or two of seniority, so "it's their turn." In that kind of culture, high performers who get passed over start looking for better opportunities elsewhere. As Steve Jobs once said, "A-plus players like to work together, and they don't like it if you tolerate B-work."

We promised our people that they would be judged and rewarded exclusively on performance, not seniority or any kind of bias. Because we worked so hard to live up to that standard, we almost never heard anyone complain about someone else getting a promotion. Almost no one was even surprised by promotion announcements.

Fast Promotions Boost Morale

Like the team splitting that we discussed in Chapter 6, fast promotions seemed like a no-brainer to us, but they contradict conventional business wisdom. So many companies intentionally keep their best people waiting for years to move up, almost daring them to quit for a better offer. They seem to think it's more cost-effective to delay promotions and hold down salaries. But if their best people get frustrated and quit, the cost of finding and training talented replacements is infinitely higher. It's another example of how traditional short-term thinking and penny-pinching haven't caught up to the new realities of work.

When we started promoting lots of associate directors and deputy directors, we saw a significant boost to morale. Some of our junior leaders even started to dress more professionally the day after being promoted. They immediately took more pride in the responsibilities that came with their new role. They wanted to look the part, to signal how much they cared and how hard they would work to justify our faith in them. That happened all the time, to the point that we could spot who had recently been promoted just by walking down the hall.

One of our most rewarding experiences at Lima One was watching our employees grow professionally and personally. We took great pride and joy in seeing them build their careers and mature as adults. Many of our fellow management team members shared our passion. Justin Thompson, who headed our marketing and inside sales teams, recalls his time with the company:

> We were able to grow from a small regional lender to a national industry leader. Our mission was often difficult and trying, but never not exciting. We helped mentor a group of young people that came into Lima One Capital with little to no professional experience, who over time were able to build careers, buy houses, and start families. It's amazing to think that a company like Lima One was able to be such a large part of so many people's lives in a relatively short period of time.

The Two Kinds of Underperformance

If someone is repeatedly underperforming, a leader's first responsibility is to figure out whether it's a competence problem or a culture/values problem. The two need to be handled very differently. Leaders need clarity about what kinds of conduct are forgivable or not forgivable, and then they need to enforce a consistent standard.

A competence problem means that someone is making an honest effort but still falling short. A Marine struggling with specific skills is always given a fair shot to achieve at the minimum required standards, often with extra help and a second, third, or sometimes fourth chance. For instance, if you were struggling to improve your accuracy on the firing range, you might get extra shooting practice with an instructor. Or, if you got out of shape and could no longer pass the physical fitness test, you'd get extra opportunities to work out. Even during recruit training, a recruit who was overweight or couldn't meet the initial fitness standards was sent to the physical conditioning platoon, where everyone had a restricted diet and additional exercise.

Even with competence problems, the Corps' patience wasn't infinite. If extra help and do-over opportunities failed, and it seemed like you were incapable of learning and improving—or unwilling to put in the required effort—you would eventually be gone. But that could take a long time. In contrast, the Corps treats honor violations as infinitely worse than competence-based underperformance. Anyone caught stealing, lying, doing drugs, or shirking their responsibilities doesn't get a second chance, let alone a fourth.

We took this distinction with us to Lima One. Employees struggling with their job skills got extra help and several chances to improve. But those who showed signs of incompatibility with our values—such as laziness, lack of teamwork, or dishonesty—would have little or no opportunity to save their jobs. We wanted them out as fast as possible, because we knew that a disconnect about values can't be fixed with teaching or coaching. The longer you allow those bad hires to go unpunished, the more likely that they will begin to degrade the workplace culture. As with cancer, early detection and fast treatment make all the difference. Unfortunately, we found that getting people off the bus quickly is another principle that's easy to declare but hard to practice.

The Danger of Procrastinating a Firing

It's very common for leaders to procrastinate pulling the trigger on firing someone, even when they know it is necessary. Maybe they like an underperforming employee for reasons that have nothing to do with performance. Maybe they're afraid of the unpleasantness of firing someone. Maybe they don't want the hassle of recruiting a replacement. In the early years of Lima One, we were guilty of all those sins, and we waited too long to fire several key people.

For instance, we once had a supernice guy we'll call Owen, whose character and work ethic were beyond reproach. He was active in the community and was very well liked and respected. He was the kind of guy you'd love to have as your next-door neighbor, because he'd always come through if you ever needed help. But he was a bad salesperson, totally incapable of closing deals. We had hired him to launch a new program, but month after month it was floundering.

Our first mistake in this scenario was hiring him too quickly because we needed someone to launch this new program. Our second mistake was waiting about five months too long before letting him go, while the program stalled out. If we had been less hesitant, everyone would have been better off, including Owen. We probably increased his anguish by making him dread being fired all those months. After he finally left, he found a different role at a more traditional company, where he's been much more successful.

Another time we were struggling to find a member of our senior management team, so we paid a ton of money to retain a fancy executive search firm. They brought us a candidate we'll call Mitch, who seemed fantastic—very smart, professional, full of good ideas. After we hired him, he quickly reorganized his team and implemented some cutting-edge new systems. Unfortunately, we had allowed our culture and values standards to drop for this hire, because we were so desperate to fill the role. Mitch was not a good cultural fit for Lima One, and we later discovered that he was dishonest.

Instead of confronting these problems immediately, we looked the other way for too long, hoping things would improve. We told ourselves that he would adapt to the culture. Also, we dreaded the thought that the search firm had been a waste of time and money, and now we would have to start over to find someone new. Those are all very common psychological responses, but they can do serious damage.

In our experience, after incompatible values are detected and discussed, an employee's behavior tends to get even worse. This leads to another failing of traditional corporate HR departments, which often focus on preventing lawsuits and therefore force leaders to jump through hoops before firing anyone. Multiple official warnings, long probationary periods, and required documentation rarely achieve anything, except delaying the inevitable.

If you're ever uncertain about whether someone should be removed from your organization, ask yourself one simple question: "Knowing what I know now, would I hire this person again if the position was open?" If the answer is no, they shouldn't be there. Confront the problem head-on, immediately. As we said in Chapter 7, if someone is shocked when they get fired, you have failed at giving them consistent, direct feedback.

Some Firings Are Harder than Others

Another example of a guilt-free firing was a sales rep we had hired to cover one of our regional markets. It soon became clear that he wasn't closing many loans, with none originating from any real estate investor clubs in his territory. When all of our field reps were in the office for training, we analyzed our loans for his region and sat down with him to ask about his performance. Hey, are you going to the real estate investor club meetings? Are you following our recommended strategies for maximizing sales? His responses didn't make sense and didn't match up with the data for his territory.

We concluded that this guy was almost never leaving his house. He wasn't going to any Real Estate Investors Association meetings or calling on local real estate attorneys to build up his referral network. He was trying to skate by with minimal work and lying to cover his tracks. Our questions got him to confess and apologize. He begged for a second chance, but we couldn't give him one.

On the other hand, some firings are exceptionally hard and might make you second-guess your decision long after the fact. This is especially true when someone's commitment to the company has diminished significantly, but you find it hard to accept that the person is no longer a top performer.

Sometimes an employee's priorities change when their life circumstances change, like a marriage, divorce, or family health crisis. It seems to come up most often with new parents, both men and women. It's understandable that the huge milestone of parenting can have a deep impact on someone's approach to their career and work-life balance. Any good leader will make reasonable accommodations to keep talent during that kind of transition. But sometimes accommodations just don't work.

This came up at Lima One with one of our early hires, who was off-the-charts outstanding on work ethic and performance during his first few years. Then he and his wife had their first child and his commitment to work began to slip. We gave him additional days off to spend time with his new child and tried to accommodate his desire to spend more time at home. The problem was that he was running a demanding department that often required overtime to close loans on schedule. Those extra hours were now impossible for him, no matter how flexible we tried to be with allowing work from home.

As part of our direct conversations about the situation, we offered him a lateral move to a less demanding department, while keeping his same salary. But he rejected that move and opted to leave with a severance package instead. It made us very sad to let him go, but since he wouldn't take the transfer, we saw no other way to keep him without sacrificing the effectiveness of a key department. With hindsight we know we had to make that decision, but it is still painful for us to have a close relationship end as it did.

Uncomfortable Decisions

Like some of the other leadership principles we have outlined, up-or-out is rarely practiced in the business world because it's not easy. It requires leaders to stick to their commitment to getting the right people on the bus and the wrong people off. It also requires making some uncomfortable decisions and having some unpleasant confrontations, whether you're promoting a junior employee over a worse-performing employee with more seniority or firing someone you personally like and respect.

Nevertheless, we've seen that no other approach to talent works better in the long run to make sure that your team of killers is reaching its maximum potential.

CHAPTER 9

AVOID COMFORT-BASED DECISIONS

Dying for Mail? (JW)

On the very last day of our deployment to Ramadi, Captain Barela and I were the last two members of Lima Company to leave OPVA. We had both accumulated lots of extra stuff over seven months, mostly letters and gifts from care packages back home. We each filled two heavy sea bags and decided to drive to Snakepit to ship them home, rather than carry them.

As we were handing over our bags at the Snakepit mail station and about to pay the shipping fees, the base was attacked by insurgent mortar fire. We took shelter under a table until the shelling stopped. Captain Barela and I looked at each other under the table, and I knew we were thinking the same two things. First, if we got killed on our final day in Iraq, just because we didn't want to travel with those extra-heavy bags, that would be a truly shameful way to go. Second, we would have died violating one of the key principles we'd learned as Marine officers: *Never make comfort-based decisions.*

The Epidemic of Comfort-Based Decisions

We define a comfort-based decision as any choice that increases your comfort, or that of your subordinates, while reducing your odds of accomplishing your mission. Today's society is experiencing an epidemic of comfort-based decision making in just about every sphere, especially in business, education, politics, and family life. We see parents caving in to their kids' demands for more screen time, instead of forcing them to do their homework or play outside. We see coaches no longer developing young athletes' fundamental skills, and merely scrimmaging with their teams.

We also see business leaders neglecting to hold employees accountable to expectations, until an organization's official standards become mere empty words and the culture sinks into mediocrity. We believe the underlying reason why so many decisions are comfort-based in the corporate world is that leaders and authority figures want to be liked more than they want to be respected. They want to accomplish their missions, but they also hate saying no. They'd rather be friends with their subordinates instead of authority figures who enforce rules and uphold high standards.

A big part of leadership is convincing people to put their best possible effort into accomplishing a mission that they might otherwise half-ass or skip entirely. It means pushing people beyond their comfort zone, physically, mentally, and emotionally. Leadership requires teaching people how to show grit in the face of adversity, and how to push through fear—whether it's the fear of death in combat, the fear of blowing a sales call, or the fear of failing a fourth-grade math test.

Ultimately, leaders who default to comfort-based decisions, or allow their subordinates to, are selfish and weak. They choose to avoid conflict and inconvenience even if it hurts the people under their care. Good leaders nurture the character of their charges by avoiding comfort-based decisions. As parents, they hold their kids and teens accountable for their choices and actions, even if that leads to short-term pain, to prepare them for the real world. As coaches, they teach their players to give everything they've got and train them to hone their skills. As business leaders, they drive their employees to deliver the best possible results.

Think about iconic leaders in any field, from football coaches like Alabama's Nick Saban to CEOs like Apple's Steve Jobs. The memories people share about these leaders always sound similar:

He drove me crazy with his high standards.

She made us run drills until we got sick.

His practices were so intense—tons of drills and almost no scrimmages.

She kept talking about the mission, the mission, the mission.

When I half-assed that project, she made me redo it.

At the time I hated him, but years later I realized how much I owe him.

Like many of the strategies in this book, avoiding comfort-based decisions is easier said than done. But this isn't brain surgery. It just takes a lot of effort to develop this attitude and stick with it when times get tough. We learned that during plenty of tough times in Ramadi.

"You Will Be Amazed at What the Human Body Can Endure" (JW)

I was shocked when we first reached Ramadi and I saw the patrol schedule that Captain Barela had drawn up. It was packed with different patrols by our platoons and squads, almost around the clock, seven days a week. Captain Barela asked me for my thoughts on the schedule.

"Sir, respectfully, I don't know how that schedule is physically possible. I don't think my Marines are capable of doing that many patrols."

His reply: "Don't worry about it, Warren. You're going to hurt for a few days, but then you will be amazed at what the human body can endure."

He was right. Lima Company quickly adapted to the extreme demands of many hours on patrol. We learned to downplay our personal needs to focus on our mission. And on the rare occasions when we didn't, the importance of "no comfort-based decisions" would come back to haunt us with deadly force.

Some of the most unpopular but also most essential rules set during our deployment were designed precisely to keep us from getting killed by comfort-based decisions. For instance:

- Always wear protective gear when outside the base, regardless of how hot or uncomfortable it is.
- Keep patrols properly dispersed to minimize IED casualties.
- No unnecessary talking on patrol, so you can stay alert.
- Run across intersections.
- Keep the pressure on the enemy with a constant, visible presence in our sector. Don't surrender the initiative.

Or think about something as basic as going to sleep. In any war zone, your schedule will be extremely erratic and often disrupted. You have to get good at catching short bursts of sleep at any hour of the day or night. Boot camp, OCS, and other phases of training teach Marines how to handle sleep deprivation and bad sleeping conditions.

It was extremely hot in Ramadi, sometimes as high as 119 degrees. "Most days were bright and insanely hot," recalls Private First Class Donovan Saffo. "Nights were warm, too. You could leave a water bottle in the sun, and it would get hot enough to cook noodles." While our platoon tracked and pursued al-Qaeda cells, most of the houses and other buildings we temporarily occupied had no air-conditioning or even decent ventilation. But other than the snipers stationed at the windows, the rest of our Marines had to stay in the center of the house, as far as possible from enemy gunfire or an RPG attack. This was a nonnegotiable rule, because we'd seen what happened to other platoons when the insurgents saw them by a window.

My platoon hated sleeping in the middle of those sweltering houses with all of their gear on, including flak jacket, helmet, and bulletproof armor plates. I hated it, too. Sometimes they pushed back. "Come on, Lieutenant, give us a break. Can we just sit by the window or sleep by the window for a couple of hours?" My answer had to be no, for their own good. I had to be willing to be unpopular. We all learned to sleep in those insanely hot and stuffy circumstances.

To this day, I've found that being able to fall asleep almost anywhere within five minutes is a useful skill. Even a cramped airplane seat is more comfortable than the cement floors and dirt floors we often slept on in Iraq. One late night at Lima One's first office, which we were subleasing from a law firm, I took a power nap on the floor. The cleaning lady walked in and started screaming because she thought I was dead. Top had a good laugh at that one. But these are the sacrifices one makes to accomplish the mission.

Saving a Life with Some Extra Discomfort (JW)

One of my favorite examples of avoiding comfort-based decisions also came during our patrols in Ramadi. It doubles as an example of innovation from the bottom up, and a rebuttal to anyone who thinks Marines don't think creatively.

Staying away from the windows of a house or abandoned building that we were occupying helped protect everyone except the platoon's snipers. Those Marines had to stay at the windows with their rifles, and if the insurgents spotted our position before we spotted them, our snipers would be sitting ducks.

Then Lieutenant Clark came up with a brilliant idea. We could re-purpose the heavy, bulletproof glass of our Humvee windows to serve as portable, see-through shields. Top requisitioned extra slabs of that heavy glass, and we started carrying it on all of our patrols. Then we used the slabs to block the windows of buildings where we set up, so our snipers could see without exposing themselves.

Initially, some of our Marines complained about the extra weight and hassle of those glass slabs. You would have thought that we were asking them to hitch a car to their backs and pull it down the streets of Ramadi. Then one night we were holed up in a building when an insurgent fired right into the window where our sniper was positioned. The Humvee glass shattered, but our Marine was unharmed. After that, my platoon was happy to carry those heavy glass shields on every patrol. In fact, they were begging to get more, and so were Marines from other platoons. As Corporal Tarantino recalls, "There was more than one instance where we came back with the same number of guys we left with because we carried those Humvee windshields."

Sandbags at OPVA

Speaking of unpleasant manual labor, remember the heavy sandbags that fortified OPVA during the April 17 attack, which we described in Chapter 1? Those were another product of refusing to make comfort-based decisions.

As soon as we began using OPVA as a second base, deeper in enemy territory, we knew it needed a substantial upgrade in its security. We made everyone in the company fill sandbags as soon as they came back to Snakepit or OPVA from every patrol. It didn't matter if they had just done a two-hour vehicle patrol or an eight-hour foot patrol throughout the city. When the squad or platoon came back, first they did a debrief about any intelligence they had gathered. Then they went outside to fill and stack sandbags for another half hour. Even if it was 2:00 a.m., no one could avoid sandbag duty.

Early on, people hated it. We were always wiped-out after a patrol and debrief. But as with any order that goes against comfort, such as carrying around those heavy glass slabs, complaints usually stop as soon as people truly understand why the unpleasant conditions are necessary. The April 17 attacks made it clear why the OPVA sandbags were essential, especially as we prepared to vacate Snakepit and make OPVA our main base.

Sandbag duty is a great example of how great leaders can improve bad situations. Corporals Tomci and Tarantino started to make filling sandbags a competition between their two squads. "Usually, the suckier things got, the more enthusiastic he and I would be," says Corporal Tarantino. Corporal Tomci also used comedy during some of these competitions to lighten the mood. Dressed in an American flag bandana, with no shirt and green silkies (Marine workout shorts), Corporal Tomci resembled a combination of a 1980s rock star and a WWE wrestler. "He would attack filling sandbags with the same tenacity as Stallone or Schwarzenegger in some action movie," laughs Corporal Tarantino. "You could not be in a bad mood when Joe was just being himself. That's one of the reasons why everyone loved him."

If you look at our pictures of OPVA, you'll see that every window and every other open space was blocked by green sandbags, piled high to

Marines reinforcing their posts with sandbags at OPVA. An average sandbag weighs forty pounds.

stop incoming fire. On the top level, each sandbag was carried up three flights of stairs. We did a good enough job to protect the levees of New Orleans from a future hurricane.

Making Sacrifices Feel Worth It

Captain Barela stuck to his plan to have Lima Company patrol our sector every day. We never suspended patrols or related missions, even immediately following the loss of a Marine in action, including Corporal Tomci. "I think patrol actions probably were stepped up after that," recalls Lieutenant Clark. "Out of respect for the loss of a warrior."

This contrasted with the decisions of other company commanders in Ramadi, who routinely gave their Marines a day or two off, sometimes more, when one of their own was killed. One company in our battalion lost four Marines pretty early in our deployment, and they became

The chow hall inside OPVA, with thousands of stacked sandbags filled by Lima Company Marines for protection.

extremely cautious, cutting way back on patrols and combat operations. They essentially took a permanently defensive posture, and our battalion commander let them get away with it (perhaps making his own comfort-based decision).

You might assume that some of Lima Company's Marines may have felt unlucky to be in a company that was so proactive with patrols and missions, when they knew that others were playing it safer with a less demanding strategy. But the company felt pride in the way we did things. We were taking the fight to the enemy every day, intelligently, with a proactive, long-term counterinsurgency strategy. We refused to hunker down defensively, waiting for the enemy to attack us. Would our Marines have liked more time off? Of course. But by using the communication strategies previously described, all of the leaders in the company convinced the Marines that our overall mission really mattered and that all of our sacrifices were worth it.

A key part of inspiring sacrifices was that our Marines knew the company's officers and staff NCOs wouldn't force them to do anything that we wouldn't do ourselves. We too were sleeping in triple-digit heat in full gear, in the center of the floor of some Iraqi building. We were sharing the load and leading from the front.

The Tragic Cost of Dropping Your Guard

One of the most tragic incidents of our time in Iraq was largely the result of a comfort-based decision. It's painful for us to recount, but we feel it's important because a future NCO or young officer can learn a great deal from the mistakes of August 29, 2006. So can anyone else reading it. We hope this story will save lives, and not just on the battlefield.

In late August, with just six weeks left in our deployment, Second Platoon was charged with guarding one of the few routes into the city of Ramadi, called Entry Control Point 2 (ECP2). As vehicles, bikes, and pedestrians crossed the bridge over the Euphrates River into Ramadi, concrete barriers funneled them into a long corridor where they would be searched. It looked similar to a mandatory weigh station for trucks on an interstate in the United States.

The battalion always had a platoon at ECP2 to supervise and assist the Iraqi police, who would perform the actual searches. Now it was Second Platoon's turn. Instead of going on patrols or other missions, these Marines set up at a building next to the bridge. In theory, this was a straightforward assignment: watch ECP2 and monitor the police as they inspected vehicles. The goal was to make sure no weapons, explosives, or insurgents were smuggled over the bridge and into the city.

While the objective was simple, the assignment was miserable. ECP2's building had no ventilation and offered no relief from the 100+ degree heat. Guarding the bridge in shifts around the clock was hot, exhausting, and boring. Generators were the only power source for ECP2, but they could not provide enough electricity to run the brand-new refrigerator that was placed there. As a result, Marines had to drink water that nearly boiled under the Iraqi sun. Such conditions will wear anyone down—mentally, physically, and emotionally.

We had been warned from day one of our deployment that al-Qaeda cells were watching everything we did. Predictable behavior patterns were extremely risky. But you can imagine the temptation Second Platoon felt when an Iraqi ice truck approached the bridge every day, to make deliveries in the city. For several days, Marines from Second Platoon bought ice from the truck once it entered ECP2. Each time, their interpreter, an Arab American from Detroit named Steve, coordinated the purchase. Before August 29, every transaction had been without incident.

On that tragic day, First Squad had just taken charge of ECP2. Twenty minutes later, the ice truck came into the area to be searched. As it arrived, a fireteam leader named Corporal Christopher Tyler Warndorf went out to meet it, along with Steve. It is important to stress that Warndorf was buying the ice with the knowledge and approval of his squad leader and platoon sergeant.

At the same time, Corporal Travis Gundrum arrived at ECP2 with two vehicles carrying hot chow and entered through a different entrance, about twenty-five yards from the ice truck. Just then, Corporal Gundrum heard a huge explosion. The ice truck had exploded, in a scene that mirrored the suicide bombing from April 17.

After calling Lima Company headquarters to notify them of the attack, Corporal Gundrum and his three Marines exited their Humvees and began to check for wounded Marines. "I went around the corner where the explosion was," he recalls. "Looking around, you could see the Iraqi police doing the searches. There were body parts all over the place. There were pieces of cars all over the place."

Initially, it seemed as though only the Iraqi police had suffered casualties. But then Corporal Gundrum heard a bloodcurdling scream. As he looked in that direction, he could see another Marine bent over in anguish. Behind him, he saw another Marine wrapped in the razor wire, blown there by the explosion. It was Corporal Warndorf. Marines from Second Platoon instantly rushed to his aid, frantically trying to free him from the wire. But as they tried desperately to untangle his body, it became clear that he'd been killed instantly by the blast.

"At that point, I lost it," recalls Corporal Gundrum. "My body was still moving. I was still doing things, but my brain was somewhere else. I was just a complete emotional wreck. It was a sucker punch near the end of the deployment, and it was the worst day of my life."

We were both part of the response team that went to the explosion, and it was a truly gruesome scene. Also killed in the blast were Steve the interpreter and twelve Iraqi police.

Corporal Warndorf was a great Marine, like many in Second Platoon. Corporal Caesar Hernandez, a squad leader and close friend of Warndorf's, had the ultimate respect for him. "Tyler [Warndorf] and I were very close," he says. "He was a smart, smart guy. He absorbed everything I tried to teach him. He was very sharp with strategy and tactics. A funny dude, and the quintessential Marine." Many others throughout Lima Company had similar feelings.

Every KIA is a tragedy, but this one was especially gut-wrenching because his death was preventable. More than fifteen years later, Captain

Barela looks back on this day with extreme anguish. "In a nutshell, they made a comfort-based decision," he says. "They bought ice to have cold drinking water during the day. And we lost a Marine and an American terp [interpreter]."

"He was trying to take care of his Marines," says Corporal Gundrum. "They were in a shitty spot. It was hot. It was humid. It was gross. He knew that getting ice helps alleviate some of that suffering. He was taking care of his Marines by buying ice, and he got killed for it."

"I think we probably all made a comfort-based decision here or there and really didn't think about it," says Sergeant MacGregor of Third Platoon. "I think we all do it at some point. Sometimes you get caught. And that's when it's a horrible example." Corporal Warndorf's death was one of those horrible examples.

In tough times, when the temptation to seek comfort is highest, it can feel almost impossible to hold people accountable and inspire them to keep doing the right thing. That's when disciplined, focused leadership is most essential. We never forgot that after August 29.

Persuading Employees to Sacrifice Their Own Comfort (JW)

The biggest difference between the military and the business world, of course, is that a commanding officer can make you do things you really don't want to do. If you're ordered to fill sandbags at 2:00 a.m., you fill sandbags at 2:00 a.m. But in business, a leader can push people only up to the point that they'll quit. To lead effectively, you must create a culture where people are willing to sacrifice their own comfort voluntarily, when a situation requires it. And you need to be able to communicate why sacrifices are required.

As you'll see in the next chapter, for two years I commuted back and forth to New York to get my MBA—an example of sacrificing comfort that led directly to an invitation to pitch a room full of Credit Suisse bankers. This was in 2013, after we had struck out in our pitch to billionaire William Erbey in Miami. We were tight on capital to lend out and in frequent danger of another cash crunch. I had recently been reading a book about Steve Jobs's style of doing presentations, and I realized that our investor pitch was much too dry and unimpressive. Maybe that was why we were struggling to win over additional investors.

I decided that we needed to reinvent our slide deck from the ground up, telling the compelling story of the company, the quality of our loans, and our vision to dominate our kind of lending. We also needed to overhaul and expand our standard operating procedures (SOPs) handbook, which Credit Suisse wanted to see. Unfortunately, we had less than two weeks to prepare for that pitch, which would take place on my next trip to New York for my MBA classes.

I assembled a killer team for this essential mission: Top; our sales director, Cortney Newmans; our marketing director, Justin Thompson;

Corporal Christopher Warndorf (*far right*) talking to local Iraqi in Ramadi, Iraq, 2006.

our treasurer, Josh Woodward; and our operations director, Rankin Blair. We dropped everything else we were doing and started working eighteen-plus hours a day on our financial models, new slide deck, presentation script, and procedures handbook. It was an extremely intense two weeks.

The first Saturday of this sprint to the presentation was the Clemson-Georgia football game—a very big deal at Lima One because Cortney had played for Georgia, and Rankin and Josh were Clemson grads and huge football fans. They had all been planning to drive to Clemson Friday afternoon for a weekend of football and fun, and then return to work on Monday. Without even having to be asked, they all came to me and Top and told us that they decided to go up for the game on Saturday night and return to Greenville as soon as it was over. We worked late into the night on Friday and came back early Saturday morning. Around 4:00 p.m. on Saturday, the gang took off for the game. They were back at the office first thing Sunday morning.

Little by little, every detail of our presentation got sharper and more engaging. The others would watch Josh and me rehearse a section, to figure out where it was ambiguous or unimpressive. Then we'd work together to revise the slides and our talking points. After countless iterations over two weeks, we were very well rehearsed. Whether or not our pitch and handouts impressed those fancy New York bankers, we could feel proud that every aspect was as strong as we could possibly make it.

Josh and I flew to New York and confidently pitched Credit Suisse. It was well received, and at the end of the meeting the managing director said, "We definitely need to do a deal with you guys. Let's make this happen." Several days later they gave us a term sheet that committed Credit Suisse to investing in Lima One. That term sheet soon became the key to unlocking many other large sources of investment capital, including the Cantor Fitzgerald partner whom we would meet a few months later at that conference in Las Vegas.

That night, Josh and I went out to celebrate the team's success, calling

Top from the rooftop bar of the Gansevoort Hotel. Top wasn't with us only because he was stuck at a cheap hotel in Cleveland, fulfilling a prior commitment to another essential mission. That was his own version of avoiding a comfort-based decision, as you'll see shortly.

When I tell this story, people tend to look at me with puzzlement. Of course the owner of a startup would work twenty-hour days to ace a do-or-die presentation. That's simply what entrepreneurs do. But why would Top, Cortney, Josh, Justin, and Rankin make an equal sacrifice of their own comfort? They didn't own any equity in the company at that point. As exempt executives, they didn't even get paid for overtime.

The answer goes back to hiring for core values and thinking long-term. A true team of killers places a premium on commitment to the team's long-term mission, above their own short-term needs. Those guys instantly understood that if Lima One scored a deal with Credit Suisse, we would all benefit tremendously. It didn't matter that in the short run they were sacrificing their personal lives, including that highly anticipated weekend at Clemson, for no extra money. I told them how much I appreciated their hard work, but they weren't doing it to get gold stars from the boss. They had faith that in the long run their commitment would be rewarded—which it was, when they later got equity in Lima One's booming value.

We had a culture of expecting hard work and rewarding hard work. Top and I set the example, and people who wanted to thrive at the company mimicked us. Those who felt that our work ethic was too extreme usually left for other organizations that put a higher priority on comfort than on mission.

Morning Ops (JW)

Around the same time that Lima One was expanding rapidly, I started feeling like my days were getting too reactive. I had so many meetings, calls, and incoming emails that I was left with no time for strategic thinking and planning. I decided to try a radical solution that was the opposite of comfort based. I called it "morning ops."

Even though I'm a natural night owl, I started setting my alarm clock for 3:45 a.m. I'd roll out of bed, throw on shorts, and drive to the office by 4:00. (It was a short ride, with zero traffic at that hour.) Then I had four hours of total silence to focus on Lima One's biggest challenges and work on long-term planning. These hours became my treasured time to be fully proactive, not reacting to anyone else's needs or priorities. I could whiteboard questions like where we should raise capital next, or what new loan products we should be developing. Morning ops was about advancing the company, rather than making short-term decisions or putting out fires.

At 8:00 a.m. I'd go to the gym for a workout to clear my head and keep in shape. Then, after a shower and a change to business clothes, I'd be back at the office by 10:00 for a normal day of meetings, calls, and emails. I'd finally leave for good around 6:00 p.m. to see my wife for dinner, followed by bed around 11:30.

Admittedly, this schedule was somewhat crazy, and I'm not saying you should copy it. There are other ways to carve out time to be proactive, such as blocking certain hours to disappear to an unused office or conference room. I chose super-early mornings because of my experience with sleep deprivation in the Marines. I knew I could function on just four or five hours of sleep.

I stuck with this version of morning ops for about three years, whenever I wasn't on the road. When my first son was born, I moved morning ops to my house from 4:00 to 7:00 a.m., then helped with the baby from 7:00 to 8:30. Then I hit the gym and got to the office by 10:30. I'd leave work around 5:00 p.m. to spend more time with my wife and son, then work another couple of hours after his bedtime.

Top's schedule resembled that of a night owl, so he found his concentrated focus time in the wee hours. He'd be in the office from around 8:00 a.m. to 7:00 p.m., then go home to dinner with his wife. By 10:00 his wife would be ready for bed, and Top would go back on his laptop until 1:00 or sometimes 2:00 a.m. We used to joke that between the two of us, often the only time we were both completely offline was 2:00 to 4:00 a.m.

To repeat, we're not saying you should copy any of these schedules. But you need to find your own way to isolate blocks of time to think and plan proactively. You need a time without emails, calls, texts, or knocks on your door. This process will probably be uncomfortable, because you'll be tempted to keep going back to the never-ending flood of incoming requests and problems. But if you can find the discipline to stick to your own version of morning ops, you'll make a big step towards reaching your strategic long-term goals.

Work-Life Balance versus the Reality of Trade-offs

Work-life balance is a fairly recent invention in American life. Most people in our parents' and grandparents' generations grew up knowing that hard, sustained work is the key to success, and no one will give you anything you haven't earned. But in the last few decades, our national work ethic has declined sharply. A large group of Americans seem to have abandoned hard and focused work. They want the fruits of success without earning them the way their elders did. They want lots of time off for socializing with friends and family, hands-on parenting, "mental health days," and eight hours of sleep every night.

There's nothing wrong with any of those things. The only problem is refusing to accept that they all require trade-offs. Every goal you pursue will force you to give up on other potential goals, because no one has the time and resources to do everything. This is such a simple and even ancient idea that it shouldn't need to be spelled out, but many Americans seem to have lost sight of it.

Take the example of someone who starts a nonprofit with the purpose of improving people's lives. If that person works extremely hard at her calling, while sacrificing fun and leisure in her twenties, her organization will almost certainly be more impactful than a similar nonprofit whose leader prioritized his social calendar over the organization. But this kind of success requires resisting comfort-based decisions at every turn. Whether you start your own business or join a big company, to reach your maximum potential you will have to work extra hours, whether early in the morning, late at night, on the weekend, or some combination of these. You will take fewer vacations than your peers, and you'll go to fewer social events. Are you willing to sacrifice comfort and pleasure now to enjoy the fruits of your labor later? What are you willing to give up to maximize your unique capabilities?

Again, there's nothing wrong with deciding you want a relatively low-stress, nine-to-five career, if you'll be happy with the career outcome resulting from that decision. No one else has the right to make those decisions for you. We're just urging you to be mindful of the trade-offs that will come with your decisions. You have to prioritize what you're really trying to achieve, and consciously accept whatever comes with that choice, good and bad. What risks, financial and otherwise, are you really willing to take? What comforts are you really willing to give up?

Think about Michael Jordan, one of the most accomplished athletes in history. He honed his natural gifts by outworking every teammate he ever had, from high school to college to the NBA. Whenever anyone tried to credit his achievements to mere talent, he would get highly offended. Jordan never made comfort-based decisions, even after he had several NBA championship rings. Listen to his perspective as the role model and leader of the Chicago Bulls:

> Winning has a price. And leadership has a price. So, I pulled people along when they didn't want to be pulled. I challenged people when they didn't want to be challenged. . . . Now, if that means I had to go in there and get on your ass a little bit, then I did that. You ask all my teammates, the one thing about Michael Jordan was, "He never asked me to do something that he didn't do." When people see this, they're going to say, "Well, he wasn't really a nice guy. He may have been a tyrant." Well, that's you. Because you

never won anything. . . . That's how I played the game. That was my mentality. If you don't want to play that way, then don't play that way.*

If you choose to follow a similar path, you will have a great advantage in today's world, because so few people are willing or able to resist comfort-based decisions. As this kind of discipline becomes increasingly rare, it also becomes increasingly rewarding. And if you can lead your team to make the same effort and endure the sacrifices, the team will achieve more than any of you thought was possible.

---

* *The Last Dance*, Episode 7, ESPN, 2020.

CHAPTER 10

THINK LONG-TERM

"It's About the Cumulative Effect"

Early in our deployment in Ramadi, First Platoon and Fourth Platoon were tasked with jointly executing a mission up Ice Street, in an insurgent stronghold designated "Delta Four" on our maps. We had developed intel about a house being used as an al-Qaeda base that needed to be cleared. Concerned about the degree of danger of the mission, the commander of Fourth Platoon sarcastically questioned Top about the wisdom and value of the mission. "Gunny Thompson, do you think anything in Delta Four is worth losing a Marine?"

Top replied instantly: "Sir, there's nothing in this freaking city that is worth losing a Marine. But it's about the cumulative effect of all the missions we do. Not just one."

This summed up one of the greatest challenges of our deployment in Ramadi. Over the course of seven months, we left the relative safety of our base to conduct hundreds of missions. Some of those missions were a complete waste of time, while others were successful. But even the best patrols and civilian interactions had limited immediate impact on the security of our sector. It was easy to get discouraged about the deployment as a whole if you judged our success by the most recent mission. We knew, for instance, that even if we successfully neutralized that al-Qaeda cell on Ice Street, other insurgents would replace them somewhere else. If we thought short-term, we might ask, "What's the point? Why put in all that effort and risk the safety of our Marines?"

Fortunately, our company leadership was great at motivating Lima Company to focus on the long-term impact of our efforts, not the short-term results of any one mission. We had a strategy to win the counterinsurgency for the long run by winning the hearts and minds of Iraqi civilians, which enabled us to develop vital intelligence against al-Qaeda. We would undermine al-Qaeda's future capacity to attack Marines and civilians, and we would ultimately drive them out of Ramadi. Each patrol, each conversation with civilians, each skirmish with the enemy was one small step towards improving our sector for the long run. Every Marine bought into the belief that the long-term effect of our missions was worth all our hard work and sacrifices.

We did conduct the mission up Ice Street that night, and fortunately we didn't lose any Marines. That would be the blueprint for our entire seven-month deployment.

The Age of Instant Gratification

It's a society-wide problem that many people focus on short-term benefits and costs. We tell ourselves things like, *I have plenty of time to save, I don't need any cash reserves right now. I don't have to eat healthy this week. I can wait to work hard until the next phase of my career.* All of those statements can be true—in the short run. The problem is that one-off actions or inactions easily turn into habits. And the cumulative effect of small deeds, positive or negative, is massive. You have to start acting as if saving fifty dollars this week will lead to financial security, and not eating junk food today will improve your long-term health, and hard work now will provide for your family in a decade.

Likewise, business leaders need to focus on how their decisions today will affect the long-term health of their company, not merely this quarter's or this year's results. The very best leaders, from Sam Walton to Warren Buffett to Jeff Bezos, plan ten or twenty years ahead, and have the discipline to ignore critics who can't see farther ahead than the next earnings report.

We view the challenge of thinking long-term in two distinct buckets. The first includes any actions that are painful in the short run but will pay off in the long run, and therefore deserve your time, effort, and resources right now. The other bucket includes anything that's easy and pleasurable right now but will create big problems later on.

Having the discipline to make the right call in both kinds of situations is much easier said than done. Let's explore a series of principles for both the DO and DON'T buckets.

Do Focus on "the Duration"—Even If You Don't Have To

Before our nation's armed forces were all-volunteer, it was much easier for American military personnel to think long-term. The Greatest Generation, who volunteered or got drafted for World War II, served for what everyone called "the duration." Millions of those veterans, like our own grandfathers, were in some combination of training and deployment for three years or more. They knew that they'd stay in until the Axis powers surrendered, which shaped their day-to-day attitude and actions.

If you were a Marine fighting in a brutally hot, high-casualty battle on an island like Tarawa or Iwo Jima, you knew exactly how your sacrifices served the long-term war effort. You knew that each island recaptured would bring the United States one step closer to striking Japan itself, which equaled one step closer to going home. The same was true for the men who stormed the beaches of Normandy and then marched across Europe to bring down Nazi Germany. They had absolute clarity about the definition of victory.

Unfortunately, recent wars have lacked true clarity on how to define "winning" or "victory," which shows a total lack of leadership at the highest levels of government. As a result, Marines and other service members have a harder time focusing on long-term goals. The reasons why the United States invaded and occupied Iraq were far more controversial than our reasons for entering World War II, and no one had a simple definition of victory. As a result, our deployment to Ramadi was clouded with ambiguity from start to finish. Much like a deployment to Vietnam decades earlier, how would a Marine measure a successful stint in Iraq? The same question could be asked all the way up the chain of command.

In addition to ambiguous goals, another challenge to long-term thinking in today's military is the strict limit on the duration of combat deployments. It's good that shorter deployments reduce burnout and make recruiting easier. But when enlisted and officers know they'll be leaving a battle space in a few months, regardless of the situation, it affects their decisions. They'll be tempted to focus on quick wins to impress their superiors. They might try to neutralize as many IED layers as possible, without worrying about developing intelligence to identify the true leaders of the insurgency. We witnessed some units significantly cutting back patrols by the midpoint of their seven-month deployment. The vision of handing over the keys to the next incoming unit dominated their thoughts and their actions.

It's hard to blame individuals when the system itself incentivizes a short-term mindset, but exceptional leaders can overcome flawed incentives. In Lima Company, Captain Barela repeatedly explained to everyone that what really mattered was our long-term impact. He stressed that our strategy for weakening al-Qaeda might not pay off fully before we returned to the United States, but it was still the right path, and possibly the only path to victory.

Leaders within Lima Company also stressed the traditions and honor of the Marine Corps. We had to live up to the high standards of all those brave Marines who fought and died in places like Iwo Jima, the Chosin Reservoir, and Hue. The manner in which we fought our battles was just as important as theirs. And we, too, had to think about "the duration."

Do Be Patient with Long-Term Strategies

Captain Barela had a clear vision of what Ramadi could and should be in the long run. As we saw in Chapter 3, he was convinced that if we could cultivate trusting relationships with the local civilians and develop actionable intelligence on high-ranking al-Qaeda leaders, we could undermine and ultimately drive al-Qaeda out of Ramadi. But it would be a slow and painstaking process. Before we had evidence that our counterinsurgency strategy was working, we spent three long months conducting our census, gathering intel, and meeting with potential allies. In other words, we persevered for nearly half of our entire deployment before seeing tangible results.

One tactical example of Lima Company's commitment to playing the long game in Ramadi was our decision to clear insurgent homes with Marines, rather than neutralizing them through air support, with its far greater risk of collateral damage. According to Corporal Tarantino, who led countless missions in Ramadi as a squad leader, this decision was pivotal. "I think what we did in our area of Ramadi was ahead of its time and really profound. It was also the right thing to do. I don't think we'll ever fully understand the ripple effect of conducting ourselves as righteously as possible, given the circumstances that we were in." He specifically recalls taking fire from a house one night and having a measured response, to avoid endangering local Iraqis in the neighborhood. "I wasn't about to unleash an infantry squad and just start hosing a residential area," he says.

As we mentioned earlier, the previous battalion in our sector had called on air support to bomb such locations. They had done this fourteen times, solving the short-term problem (a house full of

Second Lieutenant John Warren
with a local Iraqi boy inside the
home of a civilian, 2006.

terrorists) while exacerbating the long-term problem (a neighborhood full of angry civilians facing collateral damage). Since the long-term damage to our credibility and trust greatly exceeded the short-term benefit and instant gratification of that bombing tactic, we completely abandoned it.

Lima Company's policy also had a positive, lasting effect on its Marines. "I think guys would be a lot more conflicted as they grew older and would have more mental problems," says Corporal Tarantino, had we not implemented our "no bombing houses" policy. "I left Ramadi knowing I did everything right by those people, and I have a free conscience. I didn't get to choose those tactics, but I am grateful for them." This sentiment is widely shared throughout the company.

Investing in civilian infrastructure represented another example of us playing the long game in Ramadi. We saw that our sector was suffering from wartime damage to its electrical plant, water treatment plant, schools, and hospitals. Captain Barela decided that if our long-term goal required the support of the Iraqis, then improving their infrastructure and giving them the supplies they needed would help accomplish that aim. He used his discretion as company commander to redirect a lot of our time and effort in that direction. For instance, he ordered Top to procure extra stationery that could be used as school supplies—pencils, notebooks, loose-leaf paper, and so on. Then we delivered the supplies to the grateful teachers in the local schools.

When the water treatment plant in our sector was a damaged, Lima Company arranged for engineers from Baghdad to come over and fix it. We were able to pay for this through reconstruction funds that had just been recently allocated. The local neighborhoods got clean running water again, and we put the word out about how that happened.

When hospitals, schools, and private homes urgently needed generators, because the Ramadi power supply was so fragile, we requisitioned more than two thousand generators along with extra gasoline to run them. This was when al-Qaeda was running a black market in Ramadi for key supplies, including generators. In addition to the PR value of the direct help we gave the civilian population, we also sent a message that they didn't need al-Qaeda to survive. Both messages were powerful.

Once again, Marines in other companies were deeply skeptical of Lima Company's approach. They thought we were so far outside the box that we had basically lost our minds. But we knew that counter-insurgency, unlike traditional forms of war, is always a slow process. History shows that it simply doesn't work if you cut corners and try do it quickly and cheaply. You can waste years playing Whac-A-Mole with terrorist cells—neutralize one, and two more pop up. You can detect and defuse IEDs on one street and see them reappear on three other streets.

The better alternative is to step back and assess the bigger picture. If you have a portion of the population that is laying IEDs because they are financially desperate, you won't win the war by killing insurgents one by one. You have to develop human intelligence systematically to identify, locate, and remove their leaders.

Do Choose the Harder Path If It Will Pay Off Later (JW)

A few years later I found it extremely tempting to focus on short-term considerations when choosing an MBA program. As a former politics major now running a finance startup, I needed to fill a big gap in my education. There were several business schools in or near Greenville that could have taught me basic finance, with minimal inconvenience. On the other hand, I had gained admission to New York University's Executive MBA program. If I accepted, I'd have to fly to New York every other week, Thursday through Sunday. I'd miss my wife and I'd miss a lot of time at Lima One, potentially when big problems would need to be addressed. It would also be much more expensive than a local graduate program, at a time when we were watching every penny.

I decided that while a local MBA could fill many of my knowledge gaps, it couldn't compare to studying at a top-ranked university in the global capital of finance. I wanted to learn from distinguished instructors and guest speakers from leading Wall Street firms. I wanted to make connections with investment bankers and fund managers. I wanted to gain credibility and respect in our industry, while also getting a great education. All of those goals were as important as the content of the actual coursework.

Realizing this, I decided to suck it up for two years, going back and forth to New York every other week. Fortunately, I had Top running Lima One in my absence. If I hadn't trusted his judgment and leadership, NYU would have been off the table as an option. Those two years turned out to be a good opportunity for Top as well, because he developed an even better feel for the industry and got experience making tough business decisions. It was another example of why it's crucial to build a team of killers; you can trust them to cover for you.

To save money, I stayed at one of the cheapest places in New York's

Financial District, the Club Quarters, at the corner of William Street and Wall Street. The first time that Top traveled to New York with me for business, I booked us two rooms at Club Quarters. He's the least high-maintenance person I know, but even Top could only shake his head in disgust: "Next time I'm happy to pay for a hotel myself, but I won't be staying there ever again."

NYU turned out to be worth it for all the reasons I envisioned—education, credibility, a network of new classmates, and some amazing professors and guest speakers. One of the most significant was a guest speaker in my second year who had become famous as one of the first analysts at a Wall Street firm (Merrill Lynch) to blow the whistle on the danger of mortgage-backed securities. He got fired for rocking the boat, but he was correct in his assessment and was soon vindicated for his unpopular observation.

I went up to him after his lecture to thank him and introduce myself. He asked, "What line of work are you in?" I explained that I had started a lending company for real estate investors, now that the big banks were too strangled by regulations to underwrite those kinds of loans. "We've got plenty of demand from borrowers but not nearly enough capital from investors," I added.

He immediately replied, "You should talk to my friend Robbin Conner at Credit Suisse. He was just talking to me about looking for opportunities in your kind of lending. He wants to learn more." Just like that, Lima One had a foot in the door of a major Wall Street firm.

After Robbin liked what he heard at our preliminary meeting, he invited me back to pitch the managing directors of Credit Suisse's structured finance department. This was the pivotal Credit Suisse pitch that we worked so hard to prepare for, as described in the previous chapter. On the big day, as I walked through a Wall Street trading floor for the first time, feeling the energy and intensity in that giant room, I felt great about my decision to go to NYU. Of course, I couldn't have predicted this exact chain of events, but focusing on the long-term benefits of an elite MBA was clearly the right move. In this case the long run just happened to be surprisingly short.

Do Take a Chance on Going Big

Entrepreneurs love to talk about hockey stick growth, but that's rare unless you have a truly revolutionary startup, like Facebook or Uber. Most flourishing businesses have a growth curve that looks more like a staircase. You go up a bit, then level off for a while. And while you keep growing, you can repeat these steps indefinitely. At Lima One, we doubled our loan originations each year. We enjoyed a lot of steps and persevered through the plateaus. The challenge is how to shorten the time between steps, so that each plateau is as brief as possible.

About one year after we landed that Credit Suisse term sheet, Lima One Capital hit a frustrating growth plateau. We weren't generating the amount of loans that we desired. It was clear that we were not reaching enough high-end, professional clients to scale to the next level.

Our best sales rep, Cortney Newmans, had been pushing us to attend the IMN Rental Property Conference in Miami, as a great way to expand our influence with investors, borrowers, and other key contacts. We resisted because it was a very expensive conference. It would cost $32,000 to rent a prominent booth and be the platinum conference sponsor. Then if we added travel, meals, and hotel rooms for ten to twelve employees, it would be closer to $50,000. It would be a huge investment for us at a time when cash was tight. Our largest marketing expense back then was probably $5,000 for sponsoring a local real estate investor association. JW, in particular, doubted that the conference would deliver a significant return on that huge investment of money and effort.

We debated the question within the management team. In the short term, we really couldn't afford to promote Lima One at that conference. But Cortney argued that if we wanted to be more visible and originate more loans, we had to take that risk. In the long run, we couldn't afford *not* to go. We put down our deposit and started planning how best to make the conference a success.

A few days before we left for Miami, one of our biggest competitors, FirstKey, shut down all its lending operations. It was backed by Cerberus, a large private equity fund that had apparently lost faith in our sector of lending. This surprising development was a huge motivator for us, because we now had a more open market with less competition. The opportunity and timing were perfect, if we could execute our plan.

The conference turned out to be a huge success. By the time we left Miami we had already locked in enough loans to cover all of our expenses from the conference. The longer-term benefits were even greater, because we started to develop lasting relationships with some of the largest and most powerful investors in our space. Additionally, the conference boosted the Lima One brand and sent a message to the industry that we were now a force to be reckoned with.

Do Park Your Pride (JW)

When we started the company, I felt strongly that we should be a direct lender to all of our customers. To get a loan from Lima One, you had to start with a Lima One sales rep or underwriter. But by 2014, we started to get a lot of pitches from loan brokers who played matchmaker between borrowers and lenders. They could see that we had developed some of the best loan programs in our category, and we were well capitalized by this point. Brokers could feel safe that their loans with us would close and they were going to get paid.

I initially hated the thought of working with brokers because I didn't think they added any real value. Lima One proudly kept our fees as low as possible and avoided what the industry calls "junk fees" as a point of differentiation from our competitors. We would show potential borrowers term sheets from our competitors that loaded up thousands of dollars of unnecessary fees, with intentionally confusing jargon like "administration fee" and "processing fee." I didn't want to diminish our low-fee reputation by tacking on any broker fees.

We had started to put out a monthly email newsletter, and one of our subscribers was a loan broker from New Jersey. After every newsletter this guy would send an aggressive reply, telling us how dumb we were not to work with brokers, and how much extra money we could make by partnering with him. One said, "As soon as you guys want to deal with brokers, let me know. I could bring you a ton of business." We told him sorry, it's our policy not to deal with brokers. But he kept pitching us, getting increasingly adversarial. We blocked his email address, but he just resubscribed to the newsletter from a new email.

Top checked this guy out on Twitter and Facebook, where he used the self-promotional handle "Hard Money Man." He clearly knew what he was doing and was originating a nonstop flow of loans. Top, Josh, and Rankin staged an intervention of sorts, to convince me that I was being too rigid and shortsighted. They said I was focusing on my short-term goal of avoiding brokers, rather than analyzing the long-term question of how Lima One could keep growing without sacrificing our standards.

Ultimately, I realized that I had to "park my pride." There was no values-driven or business-driven justification for my resolute resistance to dealing with brokers. Hypothetically, if Lima One's origination fee was 3 percent and a broker added another 2 percent for his services, there was no impact on Lima One, and our customers had already agreed to the terms. And we needed to expand into new channels to reach more customers. Our existing setup for sales and marketing was good for the short run but would only take us so far. It was time to think outside the box.

We called Hard Money Man to make peace. He invited us up to New Jersey, and we agreed to meet him on our next trip to New York. Our first impression, at the conference room we had rented in down-town Newark, was pretty negative. We were in our business suits to meet with some Wall Street bankers later that day. Hard Money Man was wearing shorts in January. He was a tall guy with a bushy goatee, an earring, and tattoos. He seemed like our polar opposite.

But as we talked through his origination process and other details, we realized that we liked him and related to him. Beneath the surface differences, he was a lot like us—an outsider working hard to build a business in a field dominated by insiders. "We were all about good service to the client, good product to the borrower, and making sure the loans closed on time," Hard Money Man says. "It was the most important part of the business. Just sticking to your word." It was another example of the importance of focusing on a person's core values and competencies rather than appearances.

We agreed to try taking on some loans that he would broker, to give it a shot. Just as Hard Money Man predicted, his impact was through the roof. Within just a few months, he brought us so much business that it took Lima One to a new level of growth and prominence. He became the test case for our broker program, which eventually led to hundreds of other brokers bringing us customers as well. Even more surprisingly, we became good personal friends. That December we even flew him down to Greenville with his wife for our blowout Christmas party, as the only outside business partner invited.

Do Teach Others to Think Long-Term (JW)

Midway through our deployment to Ramadi, word about our successful counterinsurgency strategy was starting to spread to the press. As a result, one day I was called into Captain Barela's office at Snakepit. "Warren, the company is being assigned an embedded reporter from *USA Today*. Her name is Kimberly Johnson. You are to take her on every mission and give her access to all of your conversations with local leaders. Oh, by the way, she's from South Carolina."

I met Kim and she immediately and sarcastically said, "Hello, jarhead."

"Hello, pinko commie," I replied.

She asked when she would be able to go out with us and talk to local Iraqis. I said we'd be talking with a local imam, who currently was supporting the nationalist insurgents, that same afternoon. We briefed Kim and the Marines on the mission and prepared to depart on patrol. She asked only strategic and tactical questions and showed no concern for the dangers of Ramadi. My Marines and I were impressed.

Upon entering the imam's compound, Kim was drawn immediately to a "very cute" baby goat. It was a great icebreaker with the local leader. After petting the goat and joking about taking him home, Kim settled for naming him "Humphrey." She then turned her attention to my discussion with the imam about Anbar Province and the insurgency. After some tough negotiating, the imam and I were able to reach an agreement. He would partner with us and help provide intelligence on al-Qaeda. I was elated. To show his gratitude and respect, the imam invited us back that night for dinner.

When we returned a few hours later, the imam greeted us at his gate. Kim looked around, hoping to catch a glimpse of Humphrey. He was nowhere to be found. I paid no attention at first, as I was small-talking with the imam and looking to make sure we had good security. But after a couple of minutes, Kim asked, "Where's Humphrey?" My stomach sank and I had a very bad feeling that she was not going to like the answer.

Our interpreter, Moody, asked the imam in Arabic. He answered quickly, and the interpreter translated: "Humphrey is being served." Kim looked shocked. As we were walking inside, she whispered to me, "I am not eating this meal."

I responded with, "Yes, you are. It's a huge honor that the imam invited you to dine with us, and you are not going to screw up our agreement over Humphrey." I didn't think about it at the time, but of course I had no authority over a civilian journalist. If she was a short-term thinker who made comfort-based decisions, she could have ruined everything. Fortunately, Kim grasped the long-term importance of what we were doing. She chose to participate in the meal, sealing our newly formed relationship with the imam. It also sealed my respect for and friendship with Kim. Despite *vastly* different political opinions, we have remained friends ever since.

Don't Stay in Business with Dishonest People (JW)

Our first rule of thumb in the DON'T category may be the most important of all. Don't get entangled with dishonest or untrustworthy people, no matter how much money you can make in the short run. The damage to your reputation just isn't worth it. And those types of people will burn you in the end.

You may recall that my first real estate investing business was called WCB, for Warren, Chandler, and Bates. My partners were Ret Chandler, who provided the first $1 million in investment capital, and Tom Bates, who brought industry experience and access to customers. Ret had sold his family business and was looking for startups to back. Tom had run a big lending company geared towards real estate investors but didn't survive the financial crisis. My plan was to use Ret's $1 million to underwrite short-term (six-month) loans to some of Tom's former customers. Ret would get an 8 percent return, and Tom and I would split any leftover profits.

WCB made nine loans, and over the next several months all nine began to pay off. That was an incredibly good start, and it should have launched WCB on the road to becoming a sustainable business. Ret agreed to reinvest his $1 million after those initial nine loans paid off, and I planned to raise additional capital to expand our lending.

Unfortunately, I began to have deep misgivings about both of my partners. Even though Tom had originated thousands of loans, he hadn't learned anything significant from the mortgage meltdown. His fatal flaw was that he *didn't* do everything for a reason. He kept following the old playbook, long after the financial crisis changed the game. I started to grasp why his previous business was a total failure.

Ret, meanwhile, wasn't as ethical or trustworthy as I'd initially thought. Right before our first closing since the initial $1 million investment, he informed me over the phone that he would require the agreed-upon 8 percent *plus* half of the loan origination fee. He added, "If you don't want to hurt your credibility in the market, I suggest you take the new terms and make the loan." With smoke coming out of my ears, but not wanting to let down our borrower, I accepted the new terms for the upcoming loan. But I found it completely unacceptable to break a deal with a partner that way. Any Marine who tried a move like that would become a total outcast.

I invited Ret to breakfast the following morning at Goldberg's Bagels, the same place where I had first met him. He looked utterly shocked when I said, "I want you to know that I will guard your remaining investment as if it was my father's. But I don't deal with dishonest people, so our business relationship is over." He responded that he didn't care and didn't need me anymore, because he and Tom were going to start their own lending company. Which meant that the two of them had been conspiring against me.

Severing my ties to Ret was painful, because he was my only source of capital at that point. But I was certain that in the long run, partnering with dishonest people was the road to hell. You can't compromise your principles and values, no matter how tempting it might be for short-term gain.

A few years later, I was struck by something one of Bernie Madoff's victims told the press. Madoff's hedge fund returns had been so consistently amazing, year after year, that this investor assumed Bernie was doing something shady or illegal with his investment practices. But he figured it was fine, because even if Madoff was cheating, his clients were profiting and had plausible deniability. This person never imagined that Madoff was ripping off his own clients with the largest Ponzi scheme in history. You can't trust a dishonorable person to be honorable with *you*, no matter how close your partnership seems.

Don't Cash Out Too Soon

From the earliest days of Lima One, we always spent more than the bare minimum to build our credibility. We chose reputable and experienced service providers at every turn—our accounting firm, law firm, software providers, and so on. None were cheap, but they signaled to our investors and customers that we weren't taking shortcuts. We were in it for the long haul.

Many well-intentioned entrepreneurs find their long-term resolve wavering as soon as their business starts to generate real profits. It's almost like there's a devil on one shoulder saying, "Take out half a million and live it up. Buy a boat and a fancy car! Take the vacation of your dreams!" This devil can be a lot louder than the angel on your other shoulder, urging you to reinvest your profits for long-term growth.

There's nothing morally wrong with running what people call a "lifestyle business" that pays most of its profits to the owner every year. If that's your goal, you need to make a conscious choice, accepting the fact that cashing out today will reduce your prospects for growth tomorrow. You can have a lifestyle business or a scalable business, but almost certainly not both.

Our choice was to keep doubling down and reinvesting all profits, to keep growing the business. In 2013, Lima One made about $1.7 million in profit, well beyond our expectations. In fact, it seemed astronomical. But we ignored the "cash out" devil. We each took just $70,000 salary and no bonuses. We kept driving our old cars and living in our small homes. JW didn't even buy a house in Greenville until December 2015, and Top finally purchased his home in 2016, both after four years of renting. We figured that since we were working ninety to one hundred hours a week, our homes were mostly just places to crash, not to entertain.

Fortunately, both of our wives understood our growth strategy and were our biggest supporters. They agreed that the business should be a long-term investment, not a short-term cash cow. They just wished that we could cut back on our hours. Top's wife used to tease him by saying things like "Are you free this Saturday, or will you be with your husband again?," referring to how much time he spent working with JW. But we all kept our eyes on the prize.

This was another situation where our Marine backgrounds really helped us. Neither of us had significant assets when we left the Corps. JW spent most of his savings on a diamond ring to propose to Courtney. She was really the first angel investor of Lima One Capital, because her salary supported him for many months.

You might assume that this financial situation would make us especially eager to start cashing out profits immediately. But it didn't, because our lifestyle expectations were very low following our years in the Marine Corps. A very modest apartment in Greenville was better than anything in Ramadi. Seventy thousand dollars was much better than the salary of a platoon commander. It didn't feel like such a big sacrifice to resist instant gratification.

Millions of Americans live beyond their means; people with six- and even seven-figure incomes are tempted to spend nearly every dollar they bring in. Too many of them find that when a personal emergency hits—or a national emergency like the financial crisis or Covid—they have no reserve fund and no backup plan. That's the worst kind of short-term thinking.

Since selling Lima One in August 2019, we have had opportunities to invest in several different startups and other investment funds. Incentives are important here as well. We have found that two questions can almost always determine if an investment will fail. If the entrepreneur or fund manager has obtained some type of wealth, ask them, "How much of your personal capital are you investing alongside your investors?" Often we received responses like, "We aren't exactly investing like a typical investor, but we have put a lot of our capital into the infrastructure." Translation: "None!" Our response was always, "Where are you investing your personal capital, because clearly you believe those are better opportunities?"

The second question we ask entrepreneurs who have less of a record of success and little wealth: "If we make this investment, will you take any capital out of the company?" If so, they usually do not believe in the long-term success of the company. Adam Neumann, the notorious founder of WeWork, is the greatest example of this scenario. Over the course of several investment rounds, Neumann sold close to $1 billion of his company shares, while not permitting his employees to do the same.

Don't Cheat Your Customers

We'll end this chapter with a rule that should be too obvious to require saying: don't cheat your customers, partners, or investors for short-term gain, because you may never escape the reputational damage. Unfortunately, too many business leaders still think they can get away with terrible behavior.

GEM Mining signed an eight-figure contract to host six thousand of our Bitcoin mining computers ("miners") with a server hosting company. They were building a new hosting site, where they would be responsible for hosting and maintaining our miners. This was a critical and very expensive infrastructure investment for our new company, and we chose the company based on recommendations from people we trusted.

As we kept checking in with them about the timing for when the site would be ready, they assured us that everything was on schedule. But then they began dodging us, repeatedly. We eventually learned that they had been lying to us almost from day one. Not only had they not broken ground on their new hosting site, but they also never even obtained the construction permit. It was clear that the site would never come online.

If they had been honest with us and admitted that they were way behind schedule due to internal problems, we could have made alternate arrangements for our six thousand miners. That would have been frustrating but not catastrophic. Instead, those extremely expensive machines were just gathering dust, month after month. Bitcoin mining is a very small industry, so it didn't take long for word to get around that the hosting company lied to its customers. It is no surprise that the company later filed for bankruptcy and the management team was fired by its board.

You can choose to take advantage of someone for a few bucks (or a few million bucks), but that's the worst short-term decision imaginable. Not only will that customer never deal with you again, but they probably will do everything possible to ruin your reputation. Even if you don't care about ethics or values, it's never worth it from a purely practical and profit-driven perspective. You will make far less money in the long run by being dishonest.

Conversely, even the simplest kind of long-term thinking can give you a significant competitive advantage.

CHAPTER 11

EAT LAST

Christmas at Quantico

On the morning of December 25, 1998, General Charles C. Krulak, the commandant of the Marine Corps, headed to Marine Base Quantico, the Corps' nearby base in Virginia. General Krulak was there to continue his annual tradition of delivering hundreds of Christmas cookies to Marines serving on active duty in the Washington, DC, area during the holiday. His first stop at Quantico was to check in with the officer of the day (OOD).

On every Marine base in the world, the OOD has to monitor everything going on that day and is responsible for any incidents or problems. Each barracks or unit on the base has a duty NCO on call around the clock, reporting up to the OOD. Being OOD is an additional twenty-four-hour assignment that rotates on a random schedule among all officers stationed on the base, usually up through the rank of captain. If it's your turn to serve as OOD, any day of the year, you have to serve, even if the rest of your unit has liberty.

When General Krulak arrived at Quantico with his cookies, he asked the lance corporal who greeted him who the OOD was.

"Sir, it's Brigadier General Mattis."

"No, no, no. I know who General Mattis is. I mean, who's the officer of the day today, Christmas Day?" General Krulak was starting to get frustrated.

"It's General Mattis, sir," the lance corporal repeated.

Sure enough, James Mattis soon appeared and confirmed that he was OOD. He explained that the rotation had landed on a young officer who had recently been deployed away from his wife and kids. General Mattis had volunteered to cover the young man's OOD duty so he could get away and see his family.*

Mattis later commanded the US Central Command (CENTCOM) as a four-star general and then served as secretary of defense. In his book *One Bullet Away*, former Marine captain Nathaniel Fick describes Mattis's leadership style in Afghanistan, "No one would have questioned Mattis if he'd slept eight hours each night in a private room, to be woken each morning by an aide who ironed his uniforms and heated his MREs. But there he was, in the middle of the freezing night, out on the lines with his Marines."†

A general who volunteers as OOD on Christmas and stands watch on the front lines with his freezing men exemplifies a key principle of Marine leadership: Officers Eat Last.

---

* Vanna Le, "Jim Mattis Once Pulled Christmas Duty for a Young Marine—and It's the Perfect Holiday Story," CNBC, December 21, 2018, https://www.cnbc.com/2018/12/21/why-jim-mattis-once-pulled-christmas-duty-for-a-young-marine.html.

† Nathaniel Fick, *One Bullet Away: The Making of a Marine Officer* (Boston: Houghton-Mifflin, 2005).

Eating Last in the Marine Corps

This principle is another example of how Marines do things differently than the other service branches. If you visit any Army, Navy, or Air Force base at chow time, you'll see the senior officers get their food first, followed by junior officers, staff NCOs, NCOs, and the remaining enlisted, in rank order. Eating sooner is a perk of seniority. But at any Marine chow hall, whether at a US base or a combat deployment, you'll see the opposite sequence. The enlisted get their food first, followed by NCOs, junior officers, and senior officers. The commanding officer eats last—or, if there's a food shortage, not at all.

This may sound like a minor custom, but its symbolic importance is great. Training officers to eat last is another way that the Marines stress that leadership is a responsibility, not a privilege. It's all about sacrificing your own comfort to fulfill your mission and take care of your people. This attitude builds morale and loyalty at every level, which makes any unit more effective.

Talk is cheap. It's easy to tell your subordinates that you really care about them, and that "we're all in this together." They might or might not believe your pep talks. But if you demonstrate solidarity via actions rather than words, every day and at every meal, your people will believe that you're truly looking out for them. And if you go above and beyond eating last, to make bigger sacrifices, as General Mattis repeatedly did, your subordinates will trust you with their lives.

Many of the Lima Company Marines cite Captain Barela as their best example of good leadership. As Corporal Gundrum put it:

> The best leaders lead from the front. They endure what their Marines endure. They don't ask the men under them to complete a task that they themselves are not willing to complete. They are caring and compassionate and also a fierce force to be reckoned with. They know the inside and out of all aspects of the mission and how best to accomplish it, but they don't

have a superiority complex. Even though they know they are in charge, they will hear you out and talk to you like a human being. Captain Barela was the epitome of this. I don't know a single Lima Marine that would not have followed him into the Gates of Hell to get Lucifer's horns if he had ordered us to do that.

Sharing Perks and Privileges (JW)

How does this concept apply in business? For starters, you can choose to eat last. At Lima One, whenever we had an event that included food, such as our annual pre-Thanksgiving office lunch, Top and I made sure that everyone else got their food and drinks before we took ours. You can also let other people choose food options. Lima One had a tradition, until we grew beyond about forty employees, that everyone got a cake and a party on their birthday, with the right to choose any cake from a wonderful local bakery, the Brick Street Cafe.

This led to a memorable incident when we hired a new controller, a good-natured and quiet man in his fifties, whose birthday fell early in his tenure at the company. He chose a sweet potato cake, a decision that his new colleagues used to play a small prank on him. "Hey, Merle, did you know that John *hates* sweet potatoes? He's going to be furious." Poor Merle was terrified, thinking he might catch flak for requesting a cake that the CEO hated. He apologized to me at the start of his party, and I had to reassure him that he did nothing wrong. I said something like, "This is *your* birthday, not mine, I want *you* to enjoy the cake!"

Of course, literally eating last, or eating a cake someone else chooses, is just the tip of the iceberg. Leaders can apply "eat last" to any perk or privilege that might boost morale if shared. For instance, if you have an office with assigned parking, who gets the spots closest to the door? What message would it send to rotate the best spots every month to frontline workers rather than management? Or what might happen if you make those spots a reward for outstanding contributors? Or if you eliminate assigned parking and let the first people who arrive each day park by the door?

Think about your company's travel policies. Does senior management fly business class and rent luxury sedans, while sales reps are jammed into coach and expected to rent subcompact cars?

How about vacation time? Are the top people at your organization taking six weeks off every year, while limiting frontline staff to two weeks? In nine years of working at Lima One, outside of traditional holidays, Top took only twenty-two vacation days. Total. We both made sure that we were never out at the same time, so one of us could cover any unexpected problems instead of dumping them on others. We took our responsibilities more seriously than our vacations.

We know another company whose newly appointed CEO extended everyone's work hours before and during the December holidays. But he himself was nowhere to be found that month, because he was away for his usual long vacation. Morale plunged that year.

Likewise, in the post-Covid era we see a lot of leaders expecting everyone to return to the office all or most of the time, while senior management continues to enjoy flextime or unlimited work-from-home options. It seems so obvious that those leaders are hurting their cultures and will pay the price in higher turnover—yet this happens with surprising regularity.

Think about what you can start doing to look less selfish to your people and send the message that there's no double standard. They will notice and appreciate any changes in perks or privileges, big or small.

Sharing Hardships

The flip side of sharing perks is sharing essential sacrifices. As a leader, you can't expect anyone to work harder or longer than you do without resenting you. When we polled some former colleagues at Lima One about how they interpret "eat last," the most common reply was, "Never ask your subordinates to do anything that you aren't willing to do, or at least that you haven't already done in the past." The same was true for our Marines.

That's what General Mattis did when he shared the drudgery of being OOD on Christmas. It's what JW did in Ramadi, filling sandbags at 2:00 a.m. along with everyone else in the platoon.

It's what Top did by flying to Cleveland in February to vet the local operations team, as we mentioned in Chapter 9, instead of sending someone else while he stayed warm in South Carolina or joined our big pitch in New York City. It's what we both did on many occasions at Lima One, when an unusual task required all hands on deck for grunt work, such as photocopying and collating papers to hit a filing deadline for regulatory paperwork.

One of our favorite examples of sharing hardships is Walt Ehmer, the CEO of Waffle House, whom we first discussed in Chapter 5. Since every Waffle House location stays open 24/7, every day of the year, they always need staff who are willing to work on Christmas. In fact, Christmas is their busiest day of the year, because nearly every other restaurant in most communities is closed. Many Waffle House customers come back every year.

So does Walt. Every year for his past thirty-two Christmases as a Waffle House executive, he has strapped on an apron in one of his restaurants, serving food and wiping down tables like an entry-level employee. As he told us, "Whether it's Covid, or after a storm, or Christmas, you're not going to ask people to do something you're not willing to do yourself. For me, Christmas Day is, leave the house at six in the morning and get home by midnight, or maybe one a.m."

Speaking of Walt, we were also impressed with his response to the Covid lockdowns in March 2020, which shut down about a quarter of all Waffle House locations for an extended period, for the first time in the chain's history. (The rest remained open, at least for takeout.) Thousands of workers had to be furloughed. Walt announced that to help the company get through tough times, he would voluntarily cut his own salary in half. He also urged patrons to keep supporting the employees who were still at work: "Our associates are the true heroes during this time and appreciate any order you are able to place with them."[*]

No one looks forward to a lockdown or other tough times, but in those situations, it helps morale if management shares the pain and tries to minimize suffering. "We're all in this together," says Walt. "I care about these people and their lives and their ability to make a living and their troubles. It's easier to feel that way about people when you stand next to them versus seeing their names on a report."

Sharing Prosperity (JW)

Likewise, when times are good, I've found that it's a powerful gesture to share a company's success with the people who made that success possible. Especially when a significant bonus is unexpected, not part of any legal or contractual obligation.

By 2016, Lima One had grown to a level of sustainable profitability. We weren't a struggling startup anymore, and we were well positioned for continued growth. I still owned the vast majority of the equity, having financed our growth via debt rather than selling off chunks of the company—an example of long-term thinking that we mentioned in Chapter 10. It felt like the right time to share some of that long-term value.

It was easy to list the six key leaders whose contributions to Lima One had been most essential to our success. Top, first and foremost. Cortney, who was driving sales. Rankin, our master of operations. Josh, our head of finance. Justin, who ran marketing. And Trez, who was in charge of capital markets. All had worked their butts off and committed themselves to Lima One's values and mission. All had created significant value for the company.

I divided a 25 percent equity stake among the six of them, as a

---

[*]   Helen Regan, Joshua Berlinger, Adam Renton, Ivana Kottasová, and Meg Wagner, "March 25 Coronavirus News," CNN, March 25, 2020, https://www.cnn.com/world/live-news/coronavirus-outbreak-03-25-20-intl-hnk/h_7c37f8c3 b11547354fc777c7e7cda8e5.

one-time grant rather than a gradual, multiyear award. This gift stunned them, because it was exceptionally generous for a company of our size, and it hadn't been promised as part of their contracts—it hadn't even been mentioned. They saw it the way I intended—not as mere compensation that I was forced to give, but as a sincere expression of gratitude for their contributions.

I included some formalities about how long they would have to stay to retain their equity, but I had no doubts or worries about their continued loyalty. They were already committed for the long haul and didn't need to be incentivized. But now we were bonded together even more tightly, as both a senior management team and an ownership team. We would continue to rise or fall together.

Sharing Fun

After we got back from Ramadi to Camp Lejeune in late October 2006, our battalion planned a traditional Marine Corps birthday ball for November 10. As we've mentioned, Marines take the anniversary of the Corps' founding very seriously. It's the most important date on the USMC calendar. Unfortunately, many Marine birthday balls are boring, what we called "mandatory fun." It's hard to let your hair down when a battalion commander orders you to attend a ball with mediocre food and awkward chitchat.

But then Top had an idea that Lima Company should celebrate the end of our deployment with our own private birthday ball, just for our Marines and their dates. We wanted it to be genuine fun, not mandatory fun. With only a couple of weeks to prepare, we asked Top's wife—a professional event planner—to help us out. She found a great venue in Emerald Isle, North Carolina, and set up everything else we needed. We paid for the party by asking Lima Company's officers and staff NCOs to contribute; most of us had a good amount of money saved up because it was impossible to spend our paychecks in Ramadi. We didn't ask the junior enlisted to pay anything—another example of how the "eat last" principle had become a core value. Furthermore, Top personally spent thousands of dollars out of his own pocket to cover overruns in expenses.

At first our private party was kept secret from the battalion, the regiment, and the division. Then Captain Barela, who had a strained relationship with our battalion commander, went over his boss's head to invite his boss's boss, the regimental commander of the Eighth Marines. We hand-delivered an invitation to the regimental commander, Colonel David Berger, who would later rise to commandant of the Marine Corps. He replied that he'd be there—and to our shock, he and his wife showed up at the Lima Company party. He had a blast at our party, as did everyone else.

The Power of a Great Party

A few years later, Lima Company's birthday ball became our role model for making sure that all celebrations at Lima One were truly focused on the employees, not management. We resolved to give people real fun, not mandatory fun. The last thing we wanted was the typical office holiday party, with cheap wine, generic snacks, and everyone standing around stiffly, counting the minutes until it was safe to slip out without offending the boss.

Our first Christmas season, when we had only seven employees including the two of us, we had a low-key dinner at a local high-end restaurant. By year two we were up to twelve people, still not enough for more than dinner. But by year three, we were ready to ramp up, and we wanted a party planner who knew what would please our mostly young, energetic staff. Stacy, the former bartender whom you met in Chapter 4, volunteered to help coordinate the event. We asked her to plan a party with three goals: make people feel appreciated for all their hard work; make them feel great about being part of the Lima One team; and give them a chance to blow off steam and have genuine fun. We gave Stacy a big budget and got out of her way, with no micromanaging.

She ran the project with great enthusiasm, gathering lots of input on possible venues, bands, menus, and other details. She and her team went beyond our wildest expectations. Word got around the company that this was going to be a great party, and attendance was close to 100 percent. Everyone had a blast, launching a new tradition that quickly became part of Lima One's reputation. One of the first things new employees heard from their colleagues was that we threw awesome holiday parties.

In the years that followed, as the company kept growing, the venues got fancier and the food got even better. We started hiring top local event bands, like Dan's Tramp Stamp and Steel-Toed Stilettos, to keep everyone dancing. We started handing out funny annual awards that we called the Lundies—modeled on the Dundies from the TV sitcom *The Office*. Instead of sneaking out as early as possible, people didn't want to leave. Many stuck around after the music stopped and the venue kicked us out, migrating to a local bar for an afterparty that continued well past midnight.

As word got around Greenville, we even started to get party crashers. One year a South Carolina state representative showed up, because her own office party was terrible and she'd heard that ours was epic.

We kept throwing those holiday parties, even when the expense felt like a substantial hit to our bottom line. They helped us maintain morale and team spirit. Without all the other aspects of the Lima One culture, great parties alone probably wouldn't have meant much. But as part of the overall culture, they signaled that Lima One was a place where people worked hard and played hard—and where the bosses actually walked the walk of caring about everyone.

Find Your Own Ways to Eat Last

As we've seen, a leader can practice eating last in a wide variety of ways, from choosing to sleep on frozen ground in a combat zone, to giving up the best parking spot, to sponsoring a truly joyful party. We encourage you to experiment with new tactics that make sense for your organization.

The real test for any "eat last" tactic is not how much discomfort you impose on yourself, but what message you're sending to your people. Almost anything that comes across as a sincere expression of your care and commitment will be appreciated. But anything that seems insincere will probably be shrugged off as merely an empty gesture. When in doubt, remember what Staff Sergeant Anglade said about leadership: "The best leaders put themselves in the shoes of their subordinates, and would not ask a Marine to do something they would not do, or have not done themselves. What sets them apart is gaining the respect from their Marines and knowing that their Marines will follow them through hell and back."

PART III

PUTTING IT ALL TOGETHER

CHAPTER 12

LEAD FROM THE FRONT

Marine Corporal Michael W. Ouellette
May 25, 1980–March 22, 2009

The Greatest Leader We Know

As we conclude *Lead Like a Marine*, you may be wondering if anyone really lives up to all these principles of Marine leadership. The best way we can answer that is with one final story, about one person who exemplifies Marine leadership, in the most difficult circumstances, better than anyone we've known. Corporal Michael "Mike" Ouellette was a Marine in JW's platoon in Ramadi, during the first of his three deployments with Lima Company. He then deployed as part of the same Twenty-Second Marine Expeditionary Unit (MEU) that JW served on during his deployment with Weapons Company. Mike's third deployment, to the Nawzad District of Afghanistan, ended with his death in combat on March 22, 2009.

For his extraordinary heroism he was awarded the Navy Cross, the second-highest honor any Marine can receive, behind only the

Medal of Honor. The citation read, in part, "By his bold leadership, wise judgment, and complete dedication to duty, Corporal Ouellette reflected great credit upon himself and upheld the highest traditions of the Marine Corps."* But despite that recognition, Mike isn't remotely famous. There's never been a book or movie about his life, or even a long article in a major publication.

We're sharing his story because those of us who had the honor to know him will never forget him. He lived every one of the principles we have discussed in this book. In a world full of people who lead from the rear, Mike always led from the front.

"Tons of Energy"

Mike was born in May 1980, the middle of three children, and raised in Manchester, New Hampshire. "Mike was my pain-in-the-ass little brother," jokes his older sister Stephanie. "A quintessential middle child." Raised mostly by his mother, Donna, Mike endured a rough adolescence, like many who enlist in the Marine Corps. "We did not have a great childhood," explains Stephanie. "We were very poor. We lived in housing projects. But our mom was amazing. She did the best with what she had."

Mike's father was mostly absent, battling mental illness and substance abuse. "Mike always wanted to be a better man than our father," Stephanie says. "It made him want to be a better person, to leave people better than he found them. He wanted to be a good leader, to be everything our father was not."

He didn't play organized sports in high school, but he took solace in working out and reading. He also had lively chess matches with his younger brother, Allen. "Their games would start out quietly," remembers Stephanie. "Then Mike would lose a chess piece and the next thing you know, it's like a WWF wrestling match. Somebody's jumping out a

---

*   The Hall of Valor Project, "Michael W. Ouellette," https://valor.militarytimes .com/hero/6005.

window and somebody's grabbing a broom. Just tons of energy contained in this giant human being."

After graduating from high school in 1999, Mike worked several odd jobs for the next three years, saving money and trying to figure out his life's purpose. Then he enrolled at the California Culinary Academy in San Francisco. After going hungry occasionally as a child, he had developed a passion for food and feeding the homeless. After graduation, hoping to open his own restaurant, Mike moved to New Orleans. But frustrated by a lack of quality career opportunities, and inspired by the wars raging in Afghanistan and Iraq, he decided that his calling wasn't the cooking world—it was the US Marine Corps. He enlisted on June 15, 2005.

"Super-Boot" (JW)

After thirteen weeks of boot camp at Parris Island, and an additional nine weeks at the Marine Corps School of Infantry, Mike was assigned to First Platoon, Lima Company (3/8) at Camp Lejeune. As one of ten new arrivals in my platoon, in what we called a "boot drop," he immediately stood out. Usually, new Marines look very young and scared when they first arrive. But Mike was twenty-five, older than the others, and he had a chiseled face on his six-foot, three-inch frame that made him look mature and serious. It didn't take long for him to earn the nickname "Super-boot"—a play on the traditional nickname "Boot" for a new Marine, fresh out of boot camp. It was clear that he was very strong and in shape. I remember thinking that I wouldn't want to mess with him.

It's a long-standing Marine tradition for squad leaders and fireteam leaders to choose new Marines after a boot drop. Teams were supposed to be evenly distributed, with no team stacked with the strongest new Marines. This time it took much longer than usual for the fireteams to agree on their selections, because they all wanted Mike. Even early on, his strength and personality drew others towards him. These traits, however, did not save him from the traditional indoctrination by more senior grunts. "Garner and I used to mess with them all the time," recalled Corporal Blair Paton. "We made his life uncomfortable. But he took it, and that's one of the reasons why I respected him."

Shortly before we deployed to Ramadi, we were asked to take a picture of First Platoon outside our barracks, in formation. Every platoon has what's called a guidon, a flag that displays the company and battalion ID. It's an honor to be assigned the task of holding the guidon—an honor that went to Mike for this picture, even though he had only been with us for a couple of months. (I'm next to him on the far left of this photo.)

During our deployment to Ramadi, Mike performed as well as any Marine in First Platoon. While on guard duty at Snakepit, he often manned the M240G machine gun and was in charge of the toughest post facing down Route Michigan, where insurgents were most likely to attack. When he was on patrol, Mike always carried the heaviest loads. His character was impeccable, and his courage was unmatched. Whenever I asked him how he was doing, he always responded the same way: "Sir, I am good."

He was promoted to lance corporal in Iraq and became a fireteam leader once he returned from his first deployment. I saw a bright career ahead of him, probably as a future staff NCO. Unfortunately, his upward trajectory was about to hit an obstacle.

First Platoon, Lima Company (3/8) shortly before deploying to Ramadi, Iraq, in March 2006. Second Lieutenant John Warren is on the far left. Private First Class Michael Ouellette is to Warren's right, holding the guidon.

A Test of Character (JW)

Shortly after returning to Camp Lejeune, and despite my pleas with the battalion's executive officer to stay with my platoon, I was promoted to commander of the 81mm Mortar Platoon and transferred to Weapons Company. But Mike remained in Lima Company as a fireteam leader, now responsible for training some of the new Marines who had recently joined from boot camp. He conducted his training just as his own fireteam leader had previously done with him—by preparing his Marines for war. This meant intense physical training and discipline.

Unfortunately for Mike, the Marine Corps had recently changed its policy on what was considered hazing, and a new, subpar Marine accused Mike of just that. After a brief investigation, he faced what we call a "non-judicial punishment" (NJP), which is less serious than a court-martial but still a stain on someone's record if found guilty. In my view, Mike didn't engage in any hazing. He was going the extra mile to train his Marines properly, to maximize their odds of survival in combat. There's a clear difference between hazing and hard training. I testified to his character at the trial, giving my view that Mike had stayed on the proper side of that line.

I also testified that if I ever had a son in the Marines, I would want him to be led by Mike, who cared deeply about preparing his guys for the kind of combat he had faced in Ramadi. He gave blunt and direct feedback. He never made comfort-based decisions to become more popular. He never tried to be a buddy rather than a leader. He understood that part of his responsibility was to uphold high standards, not to let things slide just to make people happy. Unfortunately, one Marine had a hard time with all of that.

At the conclusion of the NJP, the new battalion commander found Mike guilty and sentenced him to two weeks in the brig and demotion in rank, back to private first class. This finding sickened me and all of the Lima Company Ramadi veterans. "I was blown away when that happened," recalled Paton. "I thought it was ridiculous. This is one of the best guys in the company. He suffered what I think is an injustice. But then he was back in the saddle."

I spoke to Mike just before he went into the brig, and tried to reassure him. He said he didn't regret anything because he knew he had been properly training his Marines for combat. He was prepared to serve his sentence and then go back to being the best Marine he could possibly be.

One of Mike's new Marines at the time, who would later become a fireteam leader under Mike in Afghanistan, put the entire ordeal in perspective. Mike was "a little sour about it," said Lance Corporal Ryan Mosley. "But he got over it and became a squad leader and meritoriously promoted." The way Mike handled his demotion, brig time, and career setback showed true grit and strength of character. Many others would have lost their fire and just bitterly waited for their enlistment to end.

Both Lima Company and Weapons Company deployed in the Twenty-Second Marine Expeditionary Unit. Because we were on different ships during the MEU, which ran from July 2007 to February 2008, I rarely saw Mike. He did so well that he was promoted back to lance corporal and was made a squad leader, an assignment that usually went to full corporals and sergeants. He was determined to do an outstanding job as squad leader.

"A Very High-Standards Guy"

Mike's tenure as squad leader began with another boot drop. Mosley recalled, "We had them lined up like an NFL draft. We brought the whole boot drop over, and we called dibs on who had the first-round pick."

Most of the boots took one look at Mike and wanted to be in a different squad. "I remember him being very intense," says Lance Corporal Zach Rhodas. "We were all scared to death of him. I remember when he picked me, I thought, *Please don't let this guy pick me for his squad because he's going to ruin me.* I learned a lot from him, but it was hard. He was a very high-standards guy." Another new Marine had a similar feeling. "I was really hesitant about him being my squad leader at first," claims Lance Corporal Benjamin Bowden. "But then it really paid off. We definitely had the best one out of the platoon."

Despite his previous hazing accusation, Mike began training his new squad with vigor, beginning each day with intense PT. Rhodas recalls, "We were typically up two hours before all the other squads at three or four a.m., doing a thousand jumping jacks and running four or five miles." The training was harsh but necessary preparation for a combat deployment. As Bowden notes, "It was always for a reason. He would never just say, 'Do it, because I told you to do it.' He would always explain why."

Jumping jacks were added to the workout routine after Mike had his squad do research and write short essays on different US enemies like the Taliban and al-Qaeda. During one presentation, Lance Corporal Jesse Raper described how the North Korean army did 2,500 jumping jacks before breakfast. Upon hearing this fact, Mike said, "You have to be better than your enemy. So tomorrow morning, game on." The next morning, the squad formed at 4:00 a.m. for a four-mile run with 2,500 jumping jacks sprinkled throughout the morning. They finished around 5:30, before much of the company was awake. "We lived on the third deck of the barracks," recalls Lance Corporal Will Price. "We almost had to crawl up the stairs. We could barely even walk. But that was his philosophy—you have to be better than the enemy. A lot of us took that to heart, and it made our squad better."

During many training exercises, Mike had his squad pretend that the squad leader was wounded in combat. "Tactically, that's the worst possible scenario, but it was his favorite drill," recalls Raper. "He'd take himself out of the equation to see what we could do by ourselves."

On another occasion, Price was training to use a grenade on a range with Mike. After Price threw a training grenade that ricocheted off the wall and rolled underneath Mike, he assumed it was real. Mike instantly picked Price up and threw him over the wall and then jumped on the new Marine to shield him from the blast. At what appeared to be moment of disaster, his only instinct was to protect others. "I knew at that point, he was definitely there to take care of us," says Price.

As training for the deployment wore on, Mike began to show his more intellectual side to his squad. "He would read a lot," remembered one of his fireteam leaders, Mosley. "I'd see him out on the balcony of the barracks. While everybody else was drinking or doing stupid stuff, he'd have his glass of scotch and he'd be reading war books. He always said that the best way to fight an enemy is to learn about them." Several Marines also recalled Mike telling the squad about the late Corporal Joe Tomci, and the leadership traits that made him a great Marine.

While finishing up their training at Twentynine Palms, California, Lima Company was told that their expected redeployment to Iraq had been canceled. The company now was headed to the Nawzad District of Afghanistan, the site of some of that war's most brutal fighting. But Mike's squad felt fully prepared for tough combat.

At that point Mike had the option to leave the Marine Corps, because his four-year term of enlistment was ending. But he refused to leave his squad right before the biggest challenge of their lives, so he volunteered to extend his term of service to cover a third deployment. "Ouellette didn't have to go," explains Corporal Jorge Vera. "He could have stayed back and been fine about just going to Ramadi and doing their job there. He went out of his way to make sure that the Marines he trained didn't go by themselves."

The Harsh Brutality of Afghanistan

Lima Company arrived in the Nawzad District of Afghanistan in November 2008, replacing a company from Second Battalion, Seventh Marines. The main company headquarters was Forward Operating Base (FOB) Cafferata, which one Marine described as "cold and miserable." In addition to three infantry platoons and one weapons platoon, the company had attachments to include engineers, scout snipers, and half of a shock trauma platoon. They totaled around 225 Marines.

First Platoon occupied ANP Hill, a smaller base about eight hundred meters to the south of FOB Cafferata, named after the Afghan

National Police. "We only ever had two squads in ANP Hill at any one time," recalls Bowden. "One squad would do three days of post. One squad would do three days of patrols. The other three days, one of the squads would be down at FOB Cafferata running company QRF [quick reaction force]." The accommodations at both bases were sparse, but ANP Hill was even more so. For First Platoon, the three-day rotation to FOB Cafferata provided an opportunity to "eat decent and sometimes get a shower, even workout at the gym."

Lima Company saw little combat the first two months of the deployment. "It was just a standoff because of the weather," says Mosley. "It was cold. Sometimes it snowed." But this lag in fighting was only temporary. As Lima Company's commanding officer, Captain Doug Krugman, recalls:

> The enemy had ceded the district center of Nawzad, and put everything around it with pressure-plate IEDs, extremely well buried, well concealed. I thought of it as operating in a very well-laid minefield, trying to pin us in. The mission was basically just hold on to it, because it was going to take a battalion to clear and hold this place and we only had a company. My approach was never fight for ground you're going to have to give up at the end of the day, because all they're going to do is bleed for no reason. But never let the enemy rest and never let the enemy get comfortable.

One bright spot during the first two months was Mike's meritorious promotion to corporal—an honor for any Marine, but especially for him after his punishment for hazing. Lima Company's first sergeant had convinced the battalion sergeant major and commanding officer to promote him for his outstanding performance as a squad leader. Receiving the notification at night, Krugman did not want to wait until morning to tell Mike. He and Lima Company's first sergeant left FOB Cafferata and went over to ANP Hill, where Mike's squad was manning posts. Remembers Krugman, "Everybody heard his [promotion] warrant called over the radio unexpectedly. That was one of the happier moments of that deployment for me."

On New Year's Day, the harsh brutality of Afghanistan really set in when an IED exploded, killing Lance Corporal Alberto Francesconi. Taliban attacks continued to increase as the weather improved, and four additional Marines were killed over the next few months. For First Platoon, however, "there wasn't much combat," recalls Lance Corporal Brian Boehnlein. "We were up on a hill by ourselves, basically, and the rest of the company was down below in the FOB. It seemed like we were just standing post." The most memorable event came on a patrol to a nearby town, where one squad witnessed an extrajudicial stoning of several villagers. Mike also led a "raid" on his fellow Marines at FOB Cafferata to "acquire" frozen steaks and burgers he thought the company had been hoarding. Recalls one fireteam leader, "We had steaks for four or five straight nights—it was great."

For many of the Marines in First Platoon, frustration grew from not having seen combat yet during the deployment. "All the other squads had gotten in combat except for ours," recalls Raper. "I was a stupid, nineteen-year-old grunt thinking, *When are we going to see combat? When am I going to get to prove myself?*" But having already experienced a lot of combat in Ramadi, Mike had different objectives. On one occasion he told his squad, "If we don't see shit this whole time, I'd be happy with that. As long as all of you come home safe, I couldn't ask for more." But by mid-March, more and more of his Marines were itching for combat. Soon they would all get their opportunity.

The Order

March 22, 2009, was a mild and crystal-clear day. Mike's squad was completing a rotation as the quick reaction force at FOB Cafferata. Early that morning, Captain Jessica Hawkins (a helicopter pilot) and Captain Ralph Tompkins (her gunner) took off in their Cobra attack helicopter from a larger nearby base, Camp Bastion. Hawkins had recently been promoted to section lead for her squadron and was responding to two squads of Lima Company Marines who were taking fire from Taliban forces about two kilometers from FOB Cafferata, following an early morning attack on the Taliban. Seeing enemy troops, Hawkins and Tompkins sent a Hellfire missile down a manhole cover to suppress their fires. "They had an underground network there," explains Tompkins. "We shot the Hellfire into the hole and the Marines stopped taking fire." This allowed the Marines of Lima Company to return to base without issue.

Shortly after, the Lima Company commander, Krugman, ordered Mike's squad to wake up early and conduct a foot patrol to the site of the Cobra Hellfire strike, so they could do a battle damage assessment (BDA) on the bunker and report on any enemy casualties. Recalls Krugman, "The battalion commander wanted a BDA and wanted to recover enemy remains and enemy weapons. But it was my order. I can't blame anybody else for that one." His risk assessment was that the squad could pull off the BDA safely.

Like any good Marine, Mike said, "Yes, sir," and briefed his squad. Bowden recalls wondering what the point of the BDA was, but adds, "None of us had any animosity to going out. We thought it was just going to be another run-of-the-mill day."

In fact, many were excited to be patrolling within the enemy stronghold known as the Purple Zone. Unlike the insurgents in Ramadi, the Taliban controlled distinct areas of land in Helmand Province and fought swiftly and aggressively when Marines ventured into those sectors. "The lines were definitively drawn," notes Paton. "It wasn't like Iraq. There were no-go areas in Afghanistan. They will fight you if you cross a trigger line. They're very disciplined about letting things move around outside of that trigger line. But if you cross it, you will get the stick." In other words, it was an extremely risky command decision to send Mike's squad into the Purple Zone for a BDA.

The squad assembled and grabbed Corporal Anthony Williams, a combat engineer whose specialty was sweeping for potential IEDs with a metal detector. Williams was a replacement who had not worked with Mike and his men. Many infantry Marines felt sorry for the engineers accompanying them. "None of those combat engineers knew what they had gotten into," claims one Marine. "If you told them that they were going to be leading grunt patrols, sweeping for IEDs with no rifle in front of them, in a combat zone like that, that's a whole other level of nuts." No officer or staff NCO from Lima Company elected to go out with Mike and his squad.

The Patrol

Around 10:15 a.m., Second Squad left FOB Cafferata and pushed immediately north by following a large, dried-up riverbed called a wadi. Williams was in the lead, with Price following closely behind. Mike, Lance Corporal Adam Rupert, and the remaining ten Marines were dispersed behind them. In an eerie foreshadowing, Mike and Rupert were joking about who would win the lottery that day because each had named the other for $10,000 of his $400,000 government life insurance policy. The patrol then pushed out of the wadi and continued northeast through a thick tree line. "Everything was blooming," observed one Marine. "The desert was turning green with grass." By this point, the squad had traveled about 1.5 kilometers from FOB Cafferata.

They had a difficult time locating the missile strike, possibly because so many areas were charred from missiles, IEDs, and mines. The squad eventually patrolled out of the trees and came to a large grassy field about five hundred meters long. At the end of the field was a compound believed to be the final objective for the BDA. "I either told him to come back or I hinted it was time to come back," recalls Krugman, who was monitoring the patrol from company headquarters. "And he said, 'Hey, sir, there's one more thing I want to check out. It's a couple hundred meters north.' I thought, *Okay, you're the guy on the ground. I sent you to accomplish the mission, and I'm going to let you try to accomplish your mission.*"

At this point, Mike split the squad into two large teams. He ordered

Rupert's team, along with three additional Marines, to hold their current position and provide overwatch in order to protect his flank from the Taliban. Hospitalman (HN) Matthew "Doc" Nolen, the squad's only corpsman, would stay with Rupert. According to Vera, Rupert's team "stayed back to provide cover while we crossed the field and checked out the building." Mike and his team continued north, with Williams continuing to sweep for IEDs, and Mike right behind him. Having a squad leader in front, acting as the point man, is extremely rare. Mike had previously told the squad, "If anyone's going to die, it's going to be me. I wouldn't know what to do if you all died."

About one hundred meters out, the squad's objective came clearly into view. They could see a wall with an opening that they needed to pass through to get to the compound. "There was a wall into this building that had a big rubble pile," describes Mosley. "We thought that was the impact crater." Concerned about the rubble pile in the crater, Williams continued to sweep for potential IEDs, as his metal detector remained silent. He then stepped over the pile safely with Mike following behind him. But when Mike took his next step, a huge explosion rocked the squad—sending debris, smoke, and Marines into the air.

Everything went dark after the explosion. Many from the squad were disoriented, trying to figure out what happened and who was wounded. As the cloud from the IED cleared, Vera grabbed Williams, who had been blown towards the compound, and brought him back to the rest of the squad. Meanwhile, Raper heard the chilling sound of a wounded Marine. "I just heard . . . pain. I didn't know who it was. And I'm just running through it, can't see, can't hear. And then I just fall into the crater. I look over, and there's Mike."

As Raper gained clarity, Mike's situation looked critical. "I'm looking at his leg and it's gone. The other one's torn to shit. And he's like, 'Hey, is my dick all right?' I say, 'Your dick's good, bro.' He's like, 'Okay.' I throw my two tourniquets on him. And he's like, 'Get this fucking dip out of my mouth. I can't breathe.' I take the dip out and he said, 'All right, give me my radio.' And he starts calling—cool, calm, collected from that point. Just like it's game time, but this guy's got no leg." The first radio transmission reached Lima Company at 11:29 a.m.

"He Is Still on the Radio Doing His Thing"

Back at FOB Cafferata, the standby QRF, led by Corporal Daniel Hubbert, had been monitoring the patrol. Hubbert was on his fifth combat deployment with Lima Company and was described by a fellow Marine as "another guy like Ouellette. You don't want to mess with them." Hubbert's team "had everything prepped and everybody standing by, and then as soon as the IED went boom, we turned and burned, jumped in the trucks." Accompanying the QRF was Corporal Kyle Herl, driving what's known as a "doc-in-the-box"—a state-of-the-art, portable trauma center with three beds, a trauma nurse, and a surgeon. It was secured to an armored seven-ton truck.

Meanwhile, Rupert's team was still in its previous position about three hundred to five hundred meters away. Rupert heard the explosion, followed by Mosley and Vera requesting immediate reinforcements over the radio. Rupert and his team then raced through a mine-laden corridor to reach Mike and his team. "I remember we heard an explosion," states Rhodas. "And then we hear Mosley on the radio yelling, 'Rupert, Rupert, get over here! Get over right now!' So we pick up all our stuff and start running to get to their position." It is hard to overstate the bravery it took for Rupert's team to run five hundred meters without any engineer to detect IEDs for them. "Fortunately, we all made it there. We didn't have anybody sweeping for us. We didn't know what path was safe," recalls Bowden. "We didn't know if there was somebody waiting to ambush us coming in." Doc Nolen, who had also just sprinted five hundred meters through the IED field in full gear, applied one additional tourniquet to each of Mike's legs.

Seeing Mike wounded, Mosley rushed to him. "He was refusing to let us help him. He was like, 'Set up. Set up. Mosley, you got to set them up.'" And then, a fierce rain of fire flew towards Mike and his team.

"Immediately the rounds were flying downrange," recalls Mosley. "They were coming from the north, the northeast, and the east. It was full-fledged chaos."

Severely wounded, but now reunited with his entire squad, Mike took control of the situation as his Marines set into an L-shaped formation to repel any potential Taliban attack. Mosley's team fanned out at the northwest end of the L shape. Rupert's team was positioned from the northeast corner, down the east flank. Vera's team was reinforcing both flanks. Still stunned from the initial IED blast and the ensuing firefight, Williams was called out for not firing at the enemy and apologized. Mike's blunt and direct feedback stayed true to form: "Sorry, ain't cutting it, man. Get over there and shoot. We'll talk about that later."

Mike then called in his own casualty report to headquarters, which Marines call a "nine-line." Herl, now directing the doc-in-the-box, en route to Mike, vividly remembers his transmission: "I can hear the fire over the radio. Then he comes back over and says, 'Stand by for nine-line.' He starts calling it in. 'Double amputee.' I looked at my driver and I said, 'That was him. That's Ouellette. He just called in his own kill number.' And I thought, *Well, he must have screwed that up.* And then it started dawning on us. No, he didn't screw that up. He is still on the radio doing his thing, but he doesn't have any legs."

Paton recalls the confused feelings he had after hearing Mike's nine-line transmission. "The kill number was your initials backwards, followed by a four-digit number. I was thinking 'Oscar—Whisky—Mike. Oscar—Whisky—Mike?' I thought, *Wait a minute. That's Mike's initials. How can that be?* I hear, 'Urgent Surgical.' *How can those two things be true? How is he the one talking?*"

After about ten to fifteen minutes of intense fighting, the Cobra, still piloted by Hawkins, returned to the scene after refueling. Vera, with Mike's assistance, called in the air support by talking to the COC at FOB Cafferata, who relayed the messages directly to Hawkins. Tompkins, the gunner, recalls, "We knew that they were getting engaged. We knew that rounds needed to be put downrange and Hawkins set us up for the attack." At just 1,500 feet in the air, the Cobra swung into action, swooping in from southwest to northeast.

It was a "danger-close" mission, which meant Mike's squad was too close for Tompkins to fire the Hellfire missile. According to Doc Nolen, "It wasn't just danger close, it was 'stupid danger close.'" Tompkins employed the Cobra's fierce, 20mm Gatling gun, firing thirty- to fifty-round bursts into enemy positions. "They were under heavy fire," he recalls. "I knew where they were when we did the gun run."

Many Marines from Mike's squad credit Hawkins and Tompkins for saving their lives. "We were taking heavy small-arms fire," says Boehnlein. "They were just walking it in on us. I remember saying, 'It's my time. I'm done.' Then she swooped in, and she saved our asses." According to Price, "The Cobra came over and started mowing them down." Mosley agrees: "Captain Hawkins leveled the playing field. She did a hell of a job. She saved our butts." In looking back on that moment, Hawkins explains that Marine Cobra pilots "are very aware that we are providing cover for the infantry. The infantry is the main effort, and we are there to support. And then, you have the opportunity *to actually* make a difference!"

"The Last Guy Out"

At this point, the QRF team was close to Mike's position, so he ordered Mosley and his team to link up with them and clear a safe path for them to the squad's position. Mike was also coordinating directly with the QRF. "We're talking to Mike directly," says Herl. "We were getting close. He says, 'Hey, I'm going to work here, but I'm going to send out a team to clear the road so you can get closer to us.'" Williams began sweeping for IEDs to the west, across the open field, with Mosley's team following.

About three hundred meters from Mike's position, Mosley spotted the QRF and worked on the linkup with Hubbert over the radio. Meanwhile, Williams continued sweeping as they came to an opening in a wall. Concerned about a small, suspicious rock pile, Mosley had Williams sweep it; he concluded that it was safe. But as Mosley was trying to get

Hubbert's attention, Williams walked through the opening in the wall and set off another IED. After the blast, explains Mosley, "All I remember is darkness, total blackness. And I wake up and hear Rupert yelling at me on the radio. He's like, 'Mosley, are you alive? If you're alive, say something.' I'm ignoring him because I don't know what's going on."

Unhurt from the blast himself, Mosley first saw his rifleman Lance Corporal Matthew Body, whose face was bleeding profusely from shrapnel from the IED. He next saw Williams, unconscious with wounds so bad that he had no hope of survival.

Hubbert and the QRF raced to the site of the second IED blast, just as small-arms fire and mortars began hitting the area. As Herl opened his door, he was struck in the head by shrapnel from an exploding mortar round. Luckily, he quickly realized it was a flesh wound. Body and Williams were loaded into the doc-in-the-box while Hubbert, an engineer, and seven other QRF Marines headed back on foot, under heavy enemy fire, to link up with Mike and his squad.

When the QRF finally reached Mike's squad, Hubbert deployed his Marines to the north and east, where enemy fire was heaviest. He ran to Mike and found him "self-aware and conscious and well-spirited." The Cobra was still overhead, observing, so fire from the Taliban had decreased dramatically. The original plan was for Mike to be evacuated first, under the cover of fire from the rest of the Marines; however, Mike rejected that idea. "He refused to leave until he was the last one," says Doc Nolen. "He had to be the last guy out."

Gradually, the fireteams broke down from the L-shaped formation and began moving out of the area. Mike was loaded onto a stretcher carried by four Marines, and they headed back along the same path taken by the QRF. Mike and his Marines were about three hundred meters from the doc-in-the-box and QRF vehicles. Boehnlein, nicknamed Bohika, was one of the Marines carrying Mike. As they ran, Boehnlein's rifle tripod kept hitting Mike's mangled leg. After enduring the pain for a while, Mike joked, "Bohika, if that damn tripod leg hits mine one more time, I'm gonna get up out of this stretcher and beat your ass."

Recalls Boehnlein, "It was crazy. No man should be able to handle all that and still be joking." Price continued the jokes by telling Mike, "Hey, man, you're going to be all right. We'll get a wooden peg leg for you to be a pirate." Mike laughed.

As the Marines evacuated, the Taliban resumed their attack. "We were going across the field and then we started taking contact again," says Vera. "I remember launching the rest of our M203 grenades. We shot as many of those 203 rounds to that northeast corner—all we had left." It took ten minutes for Mike's squad to reach the QRF vehicles and load Mike. "He was still awake, still alert, still talking, still making jokes," says Bowden. "I think we all thought he was going to be okay. He was missing a leg, but we thought he was going to make it."

Encountering no more enemy resistance, ten minutes later the QRF reached a landing zone (LZ) where Mike, Body, and Williams would be evacuated by helicopter to the trauma center at Camp Bastion. As Mike was being loaded, Mosley went to check on him one last time. "He looked right at me and said, 'I'm proud of you guys. Tell them I'm proud of them. They did good.' I responded, 'You're gonna be all right, man. You're gonna be okay.'" Those were the last words Mike ever spoke to a member of his beloved squad. He died of blood loss shortly after reaching Camp Bastion's trauma center.

Back at the FOB, Mike's squad was exhausted, but overall in good spirits. They even continued joking about how fun Halloween would be, with Mike as a pirate. After about two hours back at the FOB, the squad was notified that their company commander wanted to see them. Krugman walked into the room and quickly but solemnly delivered the devastating news. "There's no easy way to say this. Corporal Ouellette died."

He was two months shy of his twenty-ninth birthday.

An Unforgettable Legacy

Mike's heroism and sacrifice were truly extraordinary. He faced the ultimate challenge for any leader, and he performed above and beyond anyone's expectations. For that he was awarded the second-highest possible award for bravery in combat, the Navy Cross. No one knew Mike's leadership better than the men who witnessed it firsthand, so we asked several of them to describe him:

KYLE HERL: "He is second to none. Probably the finest example and the epitome of what it means to be a Marine I've ever personally witnessed. You wouldn't have thought that anything was wrong until you looked at his legs and they were just gone. He had a job to do and did it. There was never a point where he asked for help."

RYAN MOSLEY: "Even when he was on his deathbed, we were still listening to his orders. Nobody bucked his orders. When he snatched me up, he said, 'Get your fireteam. Go link up with Hubbard.' I would not have thought to do that. I was so in the moment. If it wasn't for him, I wouldn't be here right now, and none of us would be. Every one of us in that squad are alive today because of his actions. He talked those Cobra pilots on, setting up our reverse L-shape ambush. We would have been in a standoff with the Taliban until we all got killed or ran out of ammo. He kept his cool the whole way, didn't cry, didn't complain. He didn't yell at that engineer. He didn't make any excuses for anything. He went out like a man."

BRIAN BOEHNLEIN: "When you're more worried about your men than yourself, that's what everyone wants. He was truly leading from the front. . . . He never expected us to do anything that he wouldn't have done himself."

JESSE RAPER: "I just consider myself blessed to know the scale of what a man is actually capable of. I've tried so hard in my life to be somewhat comparable to him, and I'll never, ever achieve it. He'd get care packages from his mom but wouldn't keep any of it. He'd give it to the guys. He was the big brother we never had. He never talked about himself, never bragged. It was always other people bragging about him."

DANIEL HUBBERT: "It's fantastic perseverance under pressure and the innate ability to maintain sound mind through stressful situations. He was able to keep his guys focused and deal with the scenario."

MATTHEW "DOC" NOLEN: "He's the ultimate one you want to be. He would never ask you to do something unless he would be willing to do it. I can't speak highly enough of his leadership. I'd go to hell and back with him."

ZACH RHODAS: "We were running like a well-oiled machine—putting down fires where we needed to, suppressing what we thought was a threat. And no one got shot. We made it out of there. So, it's a testament to his leadership that we all did our jobs adequately and well."

DOUG KRUGMAN: "He held the squad's perimeter in a hand-grenade-throwing contest when he was missing one leg and the other one was shredded pretty badly. He couldn't move himself. He continued to command his squad right up until they got him in the back of the ambulance. He held them all the way through the fight."

BENJAMIN BOWDEN: "After his right leg was gone, he could have just stopped, but he didn't. He was conscious. He could communicate and he continued to do what needed to be done—calling QRF, calling the nine-line. Even though he was down, he wasn't out of the fight. He continued to direct people. At any point during that whole situation, he could have just said, 'I'm tapping out. I'm done. This shit hurts. Leave me alone.' But he didn't. He just kept on going. . . . It was a tough day, but it would have been a lot worse without his guidance. He prepared us for that. And he did a great job from day one. All of the training. All of the motivational talks. All of the knowledge that he passed on to us. We wouldn't have been half the group we were without him. . . . Mike fostered a family. We weren't a squad of Marines—we were a family of Marines."

Putting It All Together

We decided to close *Lead Like a Marine* with Mike's story in part because we believe Americans should know what happened that day in Afghanistan. Both of us were blessed to know him and to witness the impact his character and courage had on everyone around him—superiors, peers, and subordinates.

We're also closing with Mike because he was the ultimate example of what Marines call "leading from the front," which is another way to summarize the principles of Marine leadership. He lived and ultimately died by every principle that we've been addressing throughout this book.

He did everything for a reason.

He built a team of killers in his squad.

He trained them for culture and values first.

He empowered his subordinates.

He practiced blunt and direct communication.

He kept improving himself to meet up-or-out standards.

He avoided comfort-based decisions.

He focused on the long-term mission.

He ate last, down to the final moments of his life, when he refused to be evacuated until his men were safe.

Was Mike a saint, or a superhero? Of course not. He made mistakes and had moments of fear and doubt, just like the rest of us. He wasn't perfect. But that's another key lesson we can draw from his example: real leaders don't have to be perfect to be highly effective.

True leadership means accepting full responsibility for your mission, taking care of your people, and living your values in your day-to-day actions. As you continue on your own journey towards becoming a true leader, we hope you will never forget those three imperatives. Everything else is essentially just filling in the details.

ACKNOWLEDGMENTS

To the Marines of Lima Company, Third Battalion, Eighth Marines, to whom this book is dedicated. Serving in Ramadi with these extraordinary men was the greatest honor of our lives. Their skill, devotion to mission, and core values are unmatched. They are best described by a Marine veteran of the Korean War, who attended their homecoming parade upon returning from Iraq and commented to John Warren: "Lieutenant, your men can't march worth a damn, but they sure look like they can fight." Without these warriors, *Lead Like a Marine* would not exist.

To our former colleagues at Lima One Capital. They propelled us on a decade-long journey that positively impacted hundreds of employees and their families, thousands of our clients, and countless communities across the country. Because of their hard work and dedication, we all jointly built an amazing company whose impact was felt far beyond our headquarters in South Carolina. In the process, we established the best office Christmas party in America.

To our current colleagues at GEM Mining, who share new and unexpected challenges with us every day.

To Keith Urbahn and Dylan Colligan, our literary agents at Javelin, for taking our story to market and advising us so well.

To Will Weisser, for helping us tell our story as clearly as possible.

To Hannah Long, our editor at HarperCollins, for believing in the value of our story, deciding to publish it, and working to improve it. She and her team have been very supportive throughout this process.

And a special thanks to the following Marines and family members of Marines for their willingness to be interviewed for the book: Emmanuel Anglade; Max Barela; Travis Bentley; Brian Boehnlein; Benjamin Bowden; Mark Carpenter; Jason Clark; Craig Corsi; William Corso; Ryan Garner; Travis Gundrum; Jessica Hawkins; Kyle Herl; Caesar Hernandez; Dan Hubbert; Doug Krugman; Camden MacGregor; Randy Moffett; Ryan Mosley; Matt Nolen; Stephanie Ouellette; Blair Paton; Michael Perez; Will Price; Jesse Raper; Zach Rhodas; Donovan Saffo; Erich Setele; Drew Sherman; Dan Tarantino; Jon Taylor; Ralph Tompkins; Jorge Vera; Ryan Walblay.

A special thanks to the following Lima One members and associates for their willingness to be interviewed for the book: Rankin Blair; Barrett Clayton; Brandy Cogsdill; Kevin Holliday; Bill McDonald; Jack McGinness; Jim McKeon; Cortney Newmans; Dustin Simmons; Diane Sugrue; Katie Summersett; Justin Thompson; Ken Vesely; Chris Wilhoit; Josh Woodward.

Special Thanks from JW

To my parents, Steve and Geri Warren, for raising me with Marine Corps values from birth.

To my two grandfathers, Harry Warren and Hydrick Zimmerman, both of whom served with distinction in the Pacific during World War II. They set a very high bar of service, values, and character for our family.

To my loving wife, Courtney, for her constant support and for encouraging me to write down my Marine Corps experiences and what I learned from them.

To my three wonderful kids—Stevie, Drew, and Cate—for being the ultimate inspiration to complete *Lead Like a Marine*.

And, finally, to Top. No better battle buddy ever existed. He is the ultimate warrior and the kind of guy you always want in your foxhole.

Special Thanks from Top

To my loving wife, Sandy, for spending all these years by my side and giving me the vision, support, and motivation I needed in tough times. It has been a wonderful ride and I look forward to growing old with her.

To my children, Justin and Kaitlyn. Nobody said it would be easy growing up with a father who was a Marine infantryman, which led to so many moves, new schools, and new neighborhoods where they had to make new friends. I am so proud of how well they persevered and grew up to become resilient and successful adults. What an awesome sight to see.

To my brother Raymond, who took care of the home front in New York when I left to see the world. I am forever grateful for his sacrifices.

To all my aunts, uncles, and cousins, for their support over the years. I treasure the time I can spend with them now.

And, finally, to JW for his friendship, and for giving me opportunities in civilian life that I never could have imagined.